the **London** **cycle** Guide

Nicky Crowther

Haynes
THE BOOK ®

Contents

Acknowledgements

Thanks go to the following for their help in working out the routes in this book:

London boroughs and neighbours

Barnet: Tanseer Sadiq, environmental services
Bromley: Deborah Barnes, traffic, and the rangers
and Ros Martin of Crystal Palace Park
Camden: Mr G Morris
City of London: Ian Simmons, engineers
Elmbridge District Council: Martin James,
countryside and land resources manager
Enfield: Mr G Ludlow, traffic engineers office
Epping Forest District Council: Mr Keasley, Paul
Hewitt and Margaret Jones
Epsom and Ewell District Council: Alan Flaherty,
highways department
Greenwich: Mr R Warhurst
Hackney: Liam Mulrooney, environmental services
Hammersmith and Fulham: Mr S Franklin
Haringey: Malcolm Smith
Harrow: Ashad Khan
Hillingdon: Bob Castelijn, transportation

Hounslow: Mr S Sidhu, principal engineer
Islington: Tony Bowen
Lambeth: Maz Khan and Angela Christie, transport
planning
Lewisham: Brian Dalton, transportation planning
Merton: Peter Thomas and Edwina Parry
Newham: Mr M Hill, engineering
Richmond: Councillor Jo Frith, Carole Rapley
Southwark: Rob Hayward, Stave Hill ecology park,
Rotherhithe, and Mr Barkatoolah, engineering
Surrey County Council: Will Ward, district engineer,
Mark Bisson, divisional engineer
Tower Hamlets: Matthew Hill, transport planner
(cycling)
Wandsworth: Mark Raisbeck, Mahmood Sadiqqi
and Adewale Adeyoyin, engineering consultancy
Westminster City: Peter McBride, senior transport
planner

Other organisations

British Waterways: Mark Blackwell, Madge Bailey
and Liz Kelly
Corporation of London, Ashtead Common: Paul
Ritchey, keeper
Corporation of London, Hampstead Heath: the
superintendent, Mr P Canneaux
Cyclists' Touring Club: Colin Palmer, off-road
access officer
Epping Forest: the superintendent Mr Besent
Groundwork Colne Valley: Paul Hodgson, Colne
Valley programme manager
Hainault Forest Country Park: Linda Herbert
Havering and Bedfords Parks: Paul Vickers
Lee Valley Regional Park: Paul Mitchell, access
officer
The London Cycling Campaign

London Docklands Development Corporation: Phil
Harrison, cycle officer
Royal Parks and Estates: Mrs Jennifer Adams,
LVO, head of commerce and inner park; Simon
Richards, Richmond Park superintendent
Sustrans: Jane Heggett (London) and Jeremy Isles
(HQ)
Thames Water: Mike Brophy, recreation manager
Trent Park: the chief ranger
Wimbledon and Putney Commons Conservators:
J A Reader, clerk and ranger

Thanks also to John and Sarah Crowther, Phil
Elms, Perry Bellisario and Katie Burgess for
their companionship and help in hunting for
clues.

Foreword

I cycle in London to beat the system. I always have. It's my little way of resisting being overwhelmed by the place, of remaining an individual.

So I started out on this book curious. Surely there isn't any pleasurable cycling in the city? You do it to make a triumph out of a necessity. If you want to enjoy riding your bike for its own sake you have to get up horribly early on a Sunday, ride into town to catch a train to somewhere in darkest Kent, or Surrey, or Sussex, or Buckinghamshire and then get home after nightfall exhausted. But ho, was I wrong.

Bred in Barnet, I remembered damming Dollis Brook as a child – we used to get to the spot by bike. I remembered a sponsored walk along the valley to Barnet town, which is now a bike path. I now live near Richmond Park, where a magnificent 11km walking/cycling path has been installed. And up the road, don't you go over a canal bridge on the way to Harlesden? Which canal is it? Where does it go? The search for clues to enjoyable Sunday bike routes in London began in earnest.

My first criterion was that the trips should be as car-free as possible. My second was that they should be good-looking and give a taste of the diversity of the city's social and natural history. Among my favourites are Tower Bridge to Greenwich and the Lee Valley rides (5 and 8): the former for the power of the river and people's countless interpretations of it, the latter for its ageless tranquillity in an area with many modern-day problems. But every ride inspired me *en route.*

Visitors should love the city-centre tours, especially along the Thames, while experienced London bikers will get most out of the country rides. Less fit or energetic cyclists can select rides from the children's list on page 8, which consists of the routes with the least traffic and the fewest slopes. If you are foremost a mountain-biker, the off-road rides in Epping Forest and around Epsom, Warlingham and Biggin Hill (numbers 16, 23, 24, 25) are the real McCoy.

I am proud to claim that every one of these 25 routes is worth riding for its own sake. But it would have been difficult to find many more without turning criminal. After all, this is a capital city of eight million people where concrete and cars rule.

In many parts of town legality lags behind reality. That someone is riding happily along the South Bank – without causing anyone any trouble – at the moment you are reading these words does not mean that the route is official. Nor does it mean that it can be comfortably published. Rights of way law was not drawn up by cyclists, so grey areas flourish and anti-cycling attitudes persist, founded on bewilderment rather than on fact. With this in mind, all the routes have been checked with the relevant authorities (local councils and other organisations). If a couple of metres of naughtiness have slipped in here or there, law-breaking was not the intention.

As a London cyclist, you have two roles to play. First, to be nice to other people not on bikes. Second, to lobby your local council for effective cycle installations and central government for the cash to pay for them. During my research it became clear that borough cycling officers are dedicated but under-resourced, and that some can be surprisingly isolated in their task of making London more cycle-friendly. As a result you get some hit-and-miss cycling facilities. Ring your town hall to find the cycling offices, befriend them, support them...

Cycling in London is on the move and becoming better co-ordinated across the boroughs. Hail the day when the 2000km London Cycle Network is complete, providing for all trips, not just leisure ones. And hail the day when Sustrans's Thames Cycle Path (from Hampton Court to Dartford) and the Lee Valley Cycle Path (from Ware in Hertfordshire to the Thames at Bow) are in place. Moves are afoot to extend the Wandle (14) and the Ravensbourne (15) routes southwards and to build a track up the Roding Valley through north-east London. Apologies, therefore, if the routes in this book are overtaken by new developments. A second edition should include the new cycling possibilities on the London map.

With that in mind, please give us some feedback. If you have suggestions for new rides or comments about these, please write in c/o Home & Leisure Division, Haynes Publishing, Sparkford, near Yeovil, Somerset BA22 7JJ. Our intention is to acknowledge all letters.

Nicky Crowther
(left in picture)
Autumn 1997

Introduction

Contrary to popular belief, there is a lot of good riding to be had in London – you just have to find it. Between the roads and buildings lie routes along the canals, through parkland and across ancient commonland that reveal a greener side to the metropolis. The 25 routes in this book alone offer 410km of enjoyable cycling, 217km of which is car-free, even in the city centre (see Ride 1). Some of the

cycling, out in the green belt in Surrey, Buckinghamshire, Essex and Surrey, qualifies as true off-road. Elsewhere, wherever possible the routes use cycle paths and back streets.

Refresh your enthusiasm for the city with this cheap, open-air method of stress-relief. Enjoy London's green and hidden depths all the more for the capital's cycle-hostile reputation.

At the Royal Observatory, Greenwich, overlooking the Queen's House and the Royal Naval College with Canary Wharf behind.

Don't let London's heavy traffic put you off riding around the capital. With assertiveness, awareness and a tad of fitness, you can claim your space on the tarmac and enjoy being in control of your journey. The numbers of people cycling in London are increasing steadily, and the London Cycling Campaign (see page 15) reports that its membership is growing rapidly each year.

There are bad and careless drivers and good cyclists. The reverse is also true. Safety depends on two factors: awareness of potential hazards and how to avoid them; and considerate cycling techniques designed to catch the attention of other drivers and help them to help you.

Cycling hazards

Left-hand bends

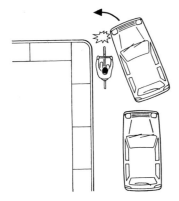

Indicate to request space as you swing round a left-hand bend so you don't get squeezed. Cars tend not to allow for your travel space. Indicate with your right arm.

Drafting

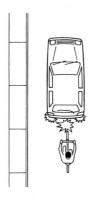

Drafting or slipstreaming vehicles is fast, furious fun, so naturally, it is dangerous. Vehicles brake more quickly than bikes, especially in the wet.

Gaps in your line of traffic

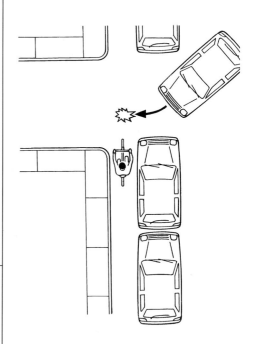

This can mean space is being left for a car outside your vision to turn into. Brake and approach with great care.

Bollards

These help pedestrians, but hinder cyclists. Anticipate that you may be squeezed, and request space by sticking out an arm in good time.

Car doors opening

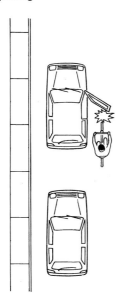

Leave 1m between you and any parked cars. Catch the driver's eye in their wing mirror.

Being crushed by lorries or buses

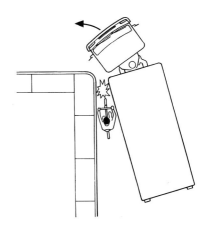

Never get on the inside of buses, coaches or lorries going left. The most frequent cause of cycling fatalities is a rider being crushed as the vehicle cuts off the apex of the corner. At lights wait behind big vehicles, and let them go ahead around corners.

GOOD CYCLING TECHNIQUES

Indicate and communicate
Use big arm movements in plenty of time to let drivers react. Make eye contact. Call out. Use a bell. Thank a helpful manoeuvre with a thumbs-up or the like.

Be well lit at night
Drivers see only lights after dark, not shadows. Reflective strips are a great aid.

Be patient and control your temper
Learning to handle the occasional idiot is part of becoming a true London cyclist.

Don't be late
Cycling takes skill, nerve and balance. If you are worried or late, you are putting yourself at risk. Keep your mind on the riding.

Get reasonably fit
Then you can flow with the traffic, not against it, get out of small spaces quicker – and enjoy yourself more.

Children and beginners

Children love to cycle, and London children can find plenty of routes to ride in this book. The information box at the start of each ride assesses its child-friendliness, based on how car-free it is, and its length, gradients and the sights to be seen on the way. Unfortunately, not one single route is completely free of traffic, although in Epping Forest you only have to dash across a few roads, not ride along any.

Adults must remain watchful of children at all times. In traffic, you should dismount to turn right, change lanes or make any manoeuvre that puts you in the way of cars. Care is especially important on canal towpaths, which can be busy and narrow.

The mountain bike routes tend to be hilly and are very hard going when muddy, which could defeat kids.

The box below lists routes considered especially suitable for children.

Most people would cycle more if they had the time to dedicate to getting fit and becoming comfortable in traffic. Several routes in this book are ideal for people who only ride occasionally, either because they are almost entirely car-free or because they are nice and flat – and short as well. Pick the routes designated for children, as they tend to be easier and avoid mixing seriously with cars.

One way of getting fitter and more skilled is simply to explore the hidden delights on your doorstep – on a bike you will discover corners you never knew existed.

Parks with cycle networks where beginners and children can ride safely include: Hyde Park, Victoria

Cycling – fun for all the family, and exercise as well.

Park (Hackney), Brockwell Park (Herne Hill), Denham Country Park (Buckinghamshire), Richmond Park, Wimbledon Common, Epping Forest, Hainault, Havering and Trent Park (Cockfosters).

Adult beginners can learn the basics of cycling in one hour at the London School of Cycling (LSC), telephone 0171-249 3779. Courses also cover riding in traffic and commuting by cycle.

LONDON BIKING FOR CHILDREN

The following rides are considered suitable for children – but read the description first to judge whether yours will enjoy the ride. Take plenty of snacks with you, be prepared to stop for rests and be encouraging.

The information box at the start of each ride lists the overground and underground stations near each route.

Overground trains

Bikes can be carried on all the local overground services in and around London. Some train-operating companies allow them at any time, some only outside the Monday–Friday morning and evening rush hours. Contact the individual train-operating companies for detailed information. Bikes usually travel free, but check with the individual train operator.

The *Rolling Cycleway*, which serves two rides (9 and 10) in this book, is an important innovation for bikers. Otherwise known as the Gospel Oak to Barking line, it runs through north and east London and has many connections with other local services. Cyclists are being actively encouraged to use it, and each train has a bike van. Ramps and cycle parking are being introduced at Blackhorse Road station, and may be installed elsewhere if the scheme proves successful. Trains run half-hourly during the day, hourly during the evenings, but there is no Sunday service between October and May. For a leaflet about the Rolling Cycleway, contact Chris Bainbridge, Hornsey Town Hall, The Broadway, Crouch End, London N8 9JJ; tel: 0181-862 1767.

The Underground

The situation on the London Underground is rather more complicated. Bikes are permitted on the 'shallow' lines, i.e. the Circle, all branches of the District, the Hammersmith & City and the Metropolitan. On the other, 'deep', lines, bikes are permitted only where the line runs above ground, not in any of the tunnel sections. In practice, this means that, with occasional exceptions, the 'deep' lines are impractical for getting to any of the rides described in this book.

Bikes can be carried on the following sections of 'deep' lines:

Bakerloo: Queens Park–Harrow & Wealdstone
Central: Leyton–Epping, Newbury Park–Hainault, Hainault-Woodford, White City–Ealing Broadway, White City–West Ruislip
Jubilee: Finchley Road-Stanmore
Northern: Colindale-Edgware, Golders Green-Hendon Central, East Finchley–High Barnet
Piccadilly: Hounslow West–Hammersmith, Cockfosters-Oakwood.

Bikes are not allowed on the Victoria Line or the East London Line, or on the Docklands Light Railway.

Bikes are not allowed anywhere during peak hours, i.e. Monday to Friday 7.30 to 9.30am and 4.00 to 7.00pm. You can take a bike on the permitted sections at all times at the weekends and on Bank Holidays.

Bikes travel free on the Underground.

Most London riding can be done at any time of year. What matters most is the weather. Wet conditions obviously make for less enjoyment and more risky riding.

The weather conditions governing the off-road riding in this book are much the same as anywhere else. Whatever the season, during and after rain the ground will be muddy and you will be grateful for your knobbly tyres.

In summer the middle of town is crammed with tourists every day, whereas out of season you will find Sundays a good time to do the inner city rides. Save the City of London ride for a Sunday if at all possible.

London is very attractive at other seasons. You can't beat a crisp winter's day in Richmond Park, when the deers' breath is foggy in the chill air.

Don't get caught out after dark in the winter without lights. Oh, and rain destroys maps and route books at great speed – pack them in something waterproof.

Stuck in the mud in Epping Forest!

Cycling on London's canals

Some of the most pleasant cycling in the capital is along the canals, which thread through interesting historical areas and offer an unusual perspective on London life. Rides 8, 9 and 21 make use of some of the best sections of towpath. Cycling on canals is a contentious issue – accidents happen from time to time, some riders are discourteous, and there is an ongoing conflict with anglers. Do your bit for cycling and ride gently on the towpaths, being friendly to everyone you meet. Give way to walkers, anglers and boaters, and dismount when the towpath gets busy. Please follow the Waterways Code for Cyclists, drawn up by British Waterways, at all times.

Bike muggings have occurred on the canals, so be sensible about keeping safe. Preferably ride in company while it is light.

Cycling is forbidden on:

• the central section of the Grand Union from Great Western Road in Westbourne Green east along the edge of Regents Park and through Camden Town to Islington tunnel in the east

• along Limehouse Cut in the East End, which is now permanently closed as it is too narrow and gets flooded

• in all the tunnels.

Find peace in the city on the towpaths (Ride 8).

A permit is required to ride the towpaths. Permits, which are annual, are available free from British Waterways, The Toll House, Delamere Terrace, Little Venice, London W2 6ND; tel: 0171-286 6101; fax: 0171-286 7306.

THE WATERWAYS CODE FOR CYCLISTS

Cycling on the towpath

• Give way to other people on the towpath and warn them politely of your approach. A 'hello' and a 'thank you' mean a lot

• Access paths can be steep and slippery – join the towpath with care

• Dismount if the towpath is busy with walkers or anglers

• Get off and push your bike if . . .
  the path gets very narrow, or beneath low bridges and alongside locks, or you encounter any other danger

• Ride at a gentle pace, in single file and do not bunch. Never race – remember you have water on one side of you

• If you are a young or inexperienced cyclist always go with a responsible adult

• Watch out for hidden mooring spikes or ropes across the path beside moored boats

• Take particular care on wet or uneven surfaces, and don't worsen them by skidding

• Never cycle along the towpath in the dark

• You are responsible for your own and others' safety

• Your bike should have a bell or hooter

• Spiky hedge trimmings can cause a puncture. We do our best to tidy them up, but recommend plastic tyre inserts just in case.

Cycling may be firmly on the transport agenda, but the increasing number of people riding in London's open spaces means that it remains controversial.

Please be courteous to everyone else using the dedicated walking/biking/riding trails. Slow down and hail people as you approach them from behind if they are in your way, and give them time to react. You can't be too careful or courteous with horses. Use the horse's reaction to you to gauge what to do: always give way, and if there is any doubt stop completely to let the horse and rider pass.

REMEMBER:
Bikers yield to horses and walkers
Walkers yield to horses

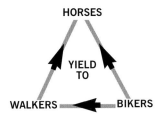

HORSES

YIELD TO

WALKERS ◄━━ **BIKERS**

Half the authorities consulted while these rides were being written mentioned complaints about people riding recklessly and freaking out pedestrians, even crashing into people on the towpaths. In Trent Park, mountain bikers have been banished from the main park to a dull piece of grassland because of blinkered riding. The response to a request to the Crown Estate to open up a piece of track for the ride around Chessington was rejected because of trouble they are having with mountain bikers in Windsor Park.

How much of this trouble results from bikers' recklessness, how much conforms with the natural rate of accidents and how much is simply in the heads of traditionally-minded authorities is unclear. What London cyclists can do to help the cause is to ride courteously and considerately with the aim of getting new lands opened up to riding, not closed off. Please stick to the Cyclists' Touring Club Off-road Cycling Code.

Bikes OK on bridleways

Rights of way law forbids cycling on footpaths. However, Section 30 of the 1968 Countryside Act states that cycling is permitted on bridleways. This is a useful fact to memorise and quote if you ever are challenged – be firm if you need to, but please remain polite.

THE OFF-ROAD CYCLING CODE

1 STAY ON THE TRAIL
Only ride bridleways & byways
Avoid footpaths
Plan your route in advance
Use the Pathfinder/Landranger maps

2 GIVE WAY TO HORSES & WALKERS
Make sure they hear you approach
Ride carefully as you pass

3 BUNCHING IS HARASSING
Ride in twos or threes

4 BE KIND TO BIRDS, ANIMALS & PLANTS
And keep your dog under control

5 PREVENT EROSION
Skids show poor skills

6 CLOSE THE GATE BEHIND YOU
(but if it's fastened open, leave it open)
Don't climb walls or force hedges

7 STAY MOBILE
Wearing a helmet may reduce the risk of head injury
Take a first aid kit
Carry enough food & drink
Pack waterproofs & warm clothes

8 TAKE PRIDE IN YOUR BIKE
Maintain before you leave
Take essential spares & tools

9 BE TIDY
Take your litter home
Guard against fire

10 KEEP SMILING

A parallel world: a cyclist enjoys a summer ride on the Lee Navigation (Ride 8).

Stop thief!

The majority of bike thefts on the streets of London are opportunist. You leave your machine outside the newsagent to pop in for a drink and it's gone when you return. So rule number one is **always lock it up.**

Use a solid steel U-lock (only heavy-duty stranded wire cables are as good), and tie the bike to something immovable like a lamp-post, railings or a bike stand. Thread the lock through the frame, the back wheel and the removed front wheel. Take off anything else that unclips: lights, pumps, water bottle and, if you are that diligent, the saddle.

Insure your bike, either as a named item, if it cost over £200 new, on your home contents policy, or separately. Take a photo of it, note the frame number, and get it postcoded at your local police station. Thousands of stolen bikes are recovered every year in London, but their owners cannot be traced.

Cycle hire and parking

There are several places in Central London where you can hire bikes. *Bikepark* has two branches, in Covent Garden and Chelsea. Their fleet of mountain bikes and hybrids are Giants and Raleighs, and they occasionally sell out on a busy Saturday, so get there early. Charges are £10 for the first day, £5 for the second, £3 per day thereafter, and £2.50 after 15 days, with a deposit of £200.

The Bikeparks also offer parking, so you can cycle into the centre of town, leave your bike on the premises, using the changing rooms if need be, and saunter round on foot or go to the theatre, knowing that your bike will be there on your return. Telephone for charges and parking times, which vary between summer and winter.

Bikepark Covent Garden is at 14 Stukeley Street, London WC2 5NH; tel: 0171-430 0083; fax: 0171-405 2834. Bikepark Chelsea is at The Courtyard, 250 King's Road, London SW3 6NT; tel: 0171-565 0777; fax: 0171-565 0779.

Another very central place to hire from is the *London Bicycle Tour Company*, which is based at Gabriel's Wharf on the South Bank, near the National Film Theatre. Here you can hire traditional and mountain bikes for £2 for the first hour, £10 for the first day, £5 for the following day, and £30 for the week. A deposit is required, for which a credit card is sufficient. The Company also offers guided tours of the London sights.

The London Bicycle Tour Company is at Gabriel's Wharf, 56 Upper Ground, London SE1 9OO; tel and fax: 0171-928 6838.

Clothing

There is rather a lot of specialist cycling gear in bicycle shops and the range can be daunting to an occasional or novice cyclist. If you are unable to go out and buy the complete outfit in one go and have to make do with what is in the wardrobe, here are general guidelines to ensure your ride is as comfortable as possible, and to prepare you for unpredictable British weather!
• Wear loose clothing that allows complete freedom of movement, such as cotton or Lycra mixes which can breathe.
• If you can buy one item of cycling gear, make it a pair of padded cycling shorts, they will provide comfort from the saddle and are designed not to chafe the skin.
• Wear a top that does not expose areas of skin, particularly the bottom of the back and the lower arms.
• Always take a waterproof; cycling in cold, wet clothes will make you miserable!
• Use glasses to protect your eyes from dust, insects and bright sunshine.
• Gloves can protect your hands, should you fall off your bicycle.

Accessories

Always wear a helmet – they can limit brain damage if you hit your head badly. A good fit is essential. The helmet should be snug and move with the scalp if you wiggle your eyebrows, but not tight enough to pinch the sides of your head. A helmet that does not fit will not offer adequate protection. A child's head is especially vulnerable, so try to get children and reluctant teenagers into the habit of wearing a helmet from the start.

A reflective belt and lights are essential, should you run out of daylight or if the weather changes dramatically. Take small change or a phonecard in case of emergencies.

A puncture repair kit, spare inner tube and bicycle pump are also essential items to carry with you on all journeys.

A bicycle computer, while not essential, is useful for seeing how far you have ridden and can tell you your maximum speed, average speed, total accumulated mileage and the time. Most have seven functions and are waterproof.

Safety precautions

Safety is, of course, a priority – particularly if you are riding with children. There is a lot that common sense will tell you. However, a few reminders are always useful.
• Always wear a helmet, even on the shortest route.
• Take great care crossing roads, particularly main A roads. Dismount and use a pedestrian crossing if there is one.
• If you are riding in poor light, or at night, make sure your lights are on and that you are wearing some reflective clothing. Ankle bands are particularly good at alerting car drivers to your presence. Also, kit your children out with a full range of reflectors.
• Check the weather forecast before you embark on a ride, especially if you are going to be out for a long time. Try to make an educated guess as to whether it is riding weather.
• Tell someone where you are going and, if possible, leave a map of the area at home.

Off-road emergencies

Because of the nature of off-road riding, it is possible that you may have to deal with an accident involving another rider. There are several things to remember:
• Place the rider in the recovery position using the minimum of movement. Keep the rider warm and place a jacket underneath their head for comfort.
• If they have sustained a head injury, do not remove their helmet unless they are bleeding severely.
• Do not give food in case they need to be operated on in a hurry.
• If you have to leave an injured rider to seek assistance, make sure that they are warm and feel able to stay awake.
• Make a note of where you have left them on your map and mark the spot with a piece of bright clothing held down by a stone or attached to a tree.
• Get help as quickly as possible.

London cycle circuits

London has three permanent cycle venues, where racing and coaching take place several times a week during the summer.

East London – The Lee Valley Cycle Circuit (previously Eastway)
Temple Mills Lane, London E15 2EN; tel: 0181-534 6085; fax: 0181-536 0959
A 1-mile tarmac track hosts road racing, criteriums (short multi-lap races) and time trials. The testing 2-mile off-road circuit and a BMX track help to cover all cycling eventualities. Fitness testing is also available.

South London – Herne Hill Stadium (see Ride 15)
Burbage Road, London SE24 9HE; tel: Cliff Barker at Southwark Leisure Services on 0171-231 9442 (no fax). Built in 1892 and the site of the cycling in the 1948 Olympics, Herne Hill is a 450m banked oval track of all-weather concrete – the fastest outdoor track in the UK. Track bikes are for hire; coaching for beginners (Saturdays 9am to 12 noon) is available all year round, and sessions for women and under-16s are held on Fridays from 6 to 8pm during the summer. Major

Courtesy of Southwark Council.

Herne Hill Stadium.

competitive events are held throughout the summer.

West London – Hillingdon Cycle Circuit
Springfield Road, Hayes UB4 (off Uxbridge Road between Southall and Uxbridge); tel: Stuart Benstead on 0181-737 7797 (no fax)
A 1-mile tarmac circuit with changing rooms. Saturday morning sessions are held for 5–16-year-olds on how to ride and race bikes.

Cycling in London is on the move (Ride 14).

The National Cycle Network

The National Cycle Network (NCN) is a major £400m Millennium Project, which will revolutionise cycling in the UK. Some 8,000 miles of signposted cycle routes will be created by 2005. Over 400 organisations are working in partnership with Sustrans, the engineering charity, to create this network of safe and attractive routes. Route 4 of the NCN includes the Thames Cycle Route which will run right through the heart of London. Sustrans' contribution to the developing LCN is scheduled for completion by the year 2000.

For information on Sustrans and the National Cycle Network, telephone 0117-929 0888 (24hr); the Sustrans web site is at: www.sustrans.org.uk.

The London Cycle Network

The London Cycle Network (LCN) is a collaboration between the boroughs to create 1500 miles of cycle-friendly roads in the capital, due for completion by the year 2005.

London Cycling Campaign

Some of the central London rides in this book were partly designed with the aid of the London Cycling Campaign map, which shows cycle paths and cycle-friendly roads. The map is recommended for London cyclists, and is available from the LCC at a cost of £4.95.

It is well worth joining the London Cycling Campaign if you want to plug into London cycling politics and culture – and get discounts at the cycle shops. The LCC magazine is full of contacts, news and advice, and is a fine vehicle of solidarity for the isolated rider. Membership also includes worthwhile benefits such as insurance and legal advice. A network of local LCC groups pursues local campaigns.

The Campaign has built itself a reputation as an authority on cycling policy and is consulted widely by government and the transport lobby. Membership is currently the highest ever, hitting 8,800 in 1998 and rising. The current membership fees are £19.50 waged; £8.50 unwaged; £12.50 waged without the magazine; £5.50 unwaged without the magazine.

Contact the LCC at 228 Great Guildford Business Square, 30 Great Guildford Street, London SE1 0HS; tel: 0171-928 7220; fax: 0171-928 2318.

EXPLANATORY NOTES AND KEY

With two exceptions (rides 4 and 15), all the routes are circular. The starting-points are at stations, landmarks or car parks – but you can of course join them wherever you choose.

The maps alongside each ride show the route in a yellow continuous line, with numbers referring to each section of description.

Dotted yellow lines indicate short-cuts, or sections where you must walk the bike, or routes under negotiation, as explained in the text.

In principle, all the routes can be ridden at any time of year, but use your common sense, especially after wet weather when off-road sections are likely to be muddy.

The refreshment stops listed are suggestions only, and do not imply any recommendation.

London Cycle Network (LCN) signs are mentioned at various points in the ride descriptions. The LCN, currently under development, is a web of roads throughout the capital being adapted and made safe for cycling as a mode of transport.

This logo appears where the route will follow route 4 of the National Cycle Network. Route 4 is planned to be open and signed in the year 2000 as part of the NCN Millenium routes (see top of this page).

Map scales: Rides 1-15 1:20,000; Rides 16-25 1:50,000

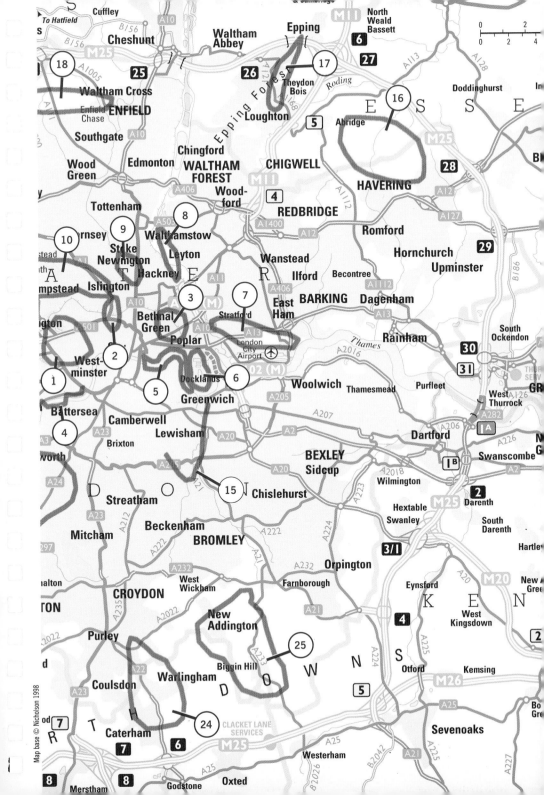

City rides

Palaces, Parks and Politics

A concentrated dose of history, politics and elegant architecture make up this short but fascinating tarmac tour through the heart of London. A long procession of world-famous sights – Buckingham Palace, the Serpentine, Marble Arch, the Zoo, Piccadilly Circus and Horse Guards Parade – are linked using four of the parkland 'lungs of London' and passing the doors of the monarch and the government.

Around Piccadilly Circus and the Haymarket, which it has been impossible to avoid, the traffic is very busy, so take care. We do not recommend the circuit for children or beginners (see below).

Distance	10km; 13km including the Serpentine circuit
Grade	Easy – flat
Bike	Preferably with smooth tyres
Suitable for children/beginners?	Not really. This is a great ride, but takes confidence on, for example, Soho's narrow roads and the lane changes. But the legal riding within Hyde Park, and down Green Park to Buckingham Palace, is suitable
Traffic and surface	15 per cent car-free, all hard-topped
Start and finish	Buckingham Palace
Overground stations	Charing Cross, Euston, Marylebone, Paddington, Victoria
Underground stations	Bayswater, Edgware Road, Great Portland Street, Paddington, St James's Park
Refreshments	Hyde Park and Regent's Park cafés, Soho
What to see	Buckingham Palace, the Serpentine, Marble Arch, Marylebone Station, Regent's Park, Soho, Piccadilly Circus, Admiralty Arch, Horse Guards Parade
What to visit	Buckingham Palace (August and September only), Cabinet War Rooms, Guards' Museum, London Zoo

1 At the pedestrian lights to the right (as you face) and north of Buckingham Palace, cross over to the entrance to Green Park and turn left up the cycle path towards Hyde Park Corner.

2 Once there, cross to Hyde Park using the subways under the roundabout – head for exit 3. There is no cycling in the subways, but a cycle crossing over Hyde Park Corner that will link with the cycle lanes in the Park is due to be constructed some time during 1998/99. Enter the park through the left-hand pedestrian arch, not the central arch, of the white stone gateway and cross the road to wide, car-free Serpentine Road.

Previous page: Start and finish this ride at Buckingham Palace.

Right: Ride beside Green Park to Hyde Park Corner.

3 (For a 3 km tour of the Serpentine, follow Serpentine Road westwards for 1.5km along the north side of the lake, then turn left on to the road, the Ring, over the lake. After another 100m, turn left again back eastwards along Rotten Row beside the horse track. Return to the junction of cycle paths at Hyde Park Corner.)

From the mouth of Serpentine Road, take the right-hand cycle path northwards and slightly uphill parallel to Park Lane. Follow this for 1km, around to the left of Marble Arch and left on to the Ring Road when the cycle path finishes.

4 After 400m turn right at the cycle sign for Paddington and cross Bayswater Road at the cycle lights. Follow the cycle path straight ahead into Albion Street. Turn right at the end (Connaught Street) and straight away left into Kendal Street. Continue straight ahead across Edgware Road and into George Street. Take the eighth left into Montagu Square, which becomes Upper Montagu Street.

5 At busy Marylebone Road cross at the pedestrian lights and continue straight ahead into Balcombe Street, then turn right (note the handsome Victorian entrance of Marylebone Station to your left) along the south side of Dorset Square and left into Gloucester Place. At the lights, stay straight ahead, Park Road, keeping the Jet petrol station on your left.

6 After 100m turn right at the zebra crossing and walk down Kent Passage – mind the pedestrians – to reach the Outer Circle of Regents Park. Cycling is not allowed in the park itself, apart from on the Inner Circle road. (It was a campaign by the Cyclists' Touring Club that got cycling permitted on the Outer Circle in 1885.)

Turn left and follow the Outer Circle three-quarters of the way round for 3km, passing London Zoo and the Regency Nash Terraces.

7 Leave the park at Marylebone Road, continue straight across at the lights into Park Crescent and turn left down Portland Place. After 100m take another left into Weymouth Street and go right at the end into Great Portland Street (following cycling signs). Take the first left into Clipstone Street (where the Telecom Tower looms). At the kink, continue straight ahead (Maple Street) and take the first right into Fitzroy Street. Continue straight ahead past the TV company HQs and eateries of Charlotte Street. Cross straight ahead at Goodge Street and continue down Rathbone Place to London's temple to shopping, Oxford Street.

8 This is the boundary of Soho, the dense quarter of cafes, theatres, media offices and strip joints. Continue straight ahead into Soho Street, round to the left of Soho Square and at the far side down Greek Street. At Compton Street, packed in the summer with cafe society, continue straight ahead to the T-junction with Shaftesbury Avenue. Turn right carefully and continue down Shaftesbury Avenue almost to Piccadilly Circus – worth a lock-up and look.

Fork left down Great Windmill Street and at the lights at the end continue straight ahead, extremely carefully, down Haymarket, which has fast traffic. At the bottom, either dismount and use the pedestrian crossings to turn right into Pall Mall, or do some nifty lane changing.

9 100m along Pall Mall, turn left into Waterloo Place and carry the bike down the wide flight of steps at the end to emerge on The Mall.

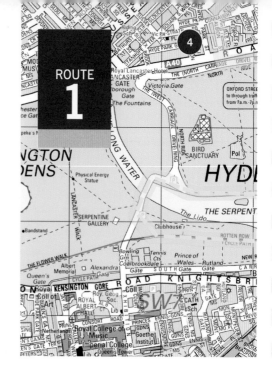

Buckingham Palace is to the right, Admiralty Arch to the left and St James's Park over the road – no cycling. Cross into Horse Guards Road nearly opposite, passing Horse Guards Parade on the left, site of many ceremonial occasions, the backside of Downing Street, home of the prime minister, and the Cabinet War Rooms, Winston Churchill's war-time headquarters.

10 Turn right at the end into Birdcage Walk, past the backside of the Home Office, the Guards' Museum and the parade ground of Wellington Barracks, home of the Foot Guards. As you approach Buckingham Palace, because of changing lanes across busy traffic, either dismount again and use the pedestrian crossings or get into the right-hand lane ready to turn right beyond the black iron gates to gain the front of the palace once more.

The 3km of riding inside Hyde Park around the Serpentine is grand for children.

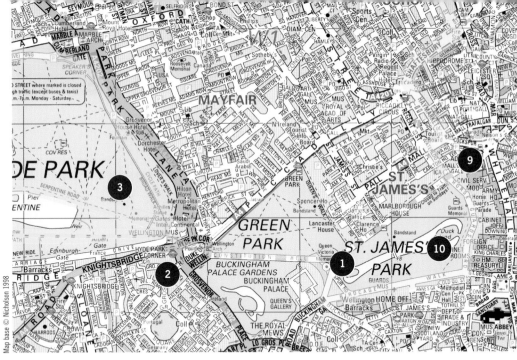

Fashion and Philosophy: Camden to Covent Garden

This central London sight-seeing road ride may be short but it cannot be done in a rush – there's just too much historical and contemporary culture to soak up, not to mention the shopping... .

Contrast the grunge of Camden Lock market with the glitz of Covent Garden via London University and the British Museum, Bedford Square, the oldest intact quadrangle in the city, and, in Lincoln's Inn Fields, the eccentric house, now museum, of architect Sir John Soane. Turn up cute Lamb's Conduit Street, and head off between the new British Library and gothic St Pancras Station for a bit of peace at Camley Street Natural Park.

Don't forget your bike lock so you can look, buy and explore at your leisure. There's a fair bit of traffic, although we use backstreets where possible, so the ride is not recommended for children or beginners.

Distance	8km
Grade	Easy – flat
Bike	Preferably with smooth tyres
Suitable for children/beginners?	Not really. Even at weekends the roads around Euston and Camden are busy, but Camley Street Natural Park is tempting, and then adults are not allowed into Coram's Fields unless accompanied by a child...
Traffic and surface	10 per cent traffic-free, all hard-topped
Start and finish	Camden Lock
Overground stations	Camden Road, Charing Cross, Euston, Farringdon, King's Cross, St Pancras, Waterloo
Underground stations	Euston Square, Farringdon, Great Portland Street, King's Cross/St Pancras, Temple
Refreshments	Camden Lock, Covent Garden, Lamb's Conduit Street
What to see	Camden Lock market, London University Senate House (built 1936), 18th-century town housing and Bedford Square (1775), former Midland Grand Hotel at St Pancras Station (1874), the new British Library
What to visit	British Museum, Camley Street Natural Park (closed Fridays), London Transport Museum, Sir John Soane's Museum

1 Begin at Camden Lock market on the bridge over the Grand Union Canal on Chalk Farm Road. After a good look around the market, walk on the pavement southwards for a short way to the traffic light junction with Jamestown Road on the right. Turn down here and take the first left into Arlington Road. Continue straight ahead for 1km, turn right into Mornington Crescent and continue to the end.

2 Here, dismount to turn right, southwards, down Hampstead Road by crossing the one-way roads on foot and picking up the cycle lane. Continue for 500m to the major junction at Euston underpass.

3 At this busy junction take the left fork over the underpass (not the 90 degrees left turn on to the spur road that joins the underpass road). Dog-leg left and right to continue southwards down Gower Street. Continue straight ahead for 1km past University College on the left, London University Senate House (seen down Keppel Street, left), through handsome 18th-century Bedford Square and near the west perimeter of the British Museum (entrance on Russell Street, left), becoming Bloomsbury Street, to the T-junction at the bottom.

4 When the Oasis Sports Centre appears in front, bend right with the one-way traffic and take the immediate left into pleasant little Endell Street, which leads to Covent Garden. (Time for a look around and a little something to eat perhaps?) Turn

Avoid tackling this ride in rush hours, and be aware that Camden Lock becomes very crowded at weekends.

Map base © Nicholson 1998

Bedford Square, the oldest intact quadrangle in London.

left at the mini-roundabout at the end into Long Acre, and continue straight ahead at the crossing with Drury Lane into Great Queen Street.

5 Go straight ahead over busy Kingsway and continue along the north side of Lincoln's Inn Fields, past Sir John Soane's house, left, which has been turned into a museum of the collector's art and artefacts. At the corner of the square, turn left northwards up the side street and dismount to walk through the passage leading out to High Holborn. Turn left and immediately take the first right up Red Lion Street.

6 Cross Theobalds Road at the end and continue straight ahead up Lamb's Conduit Street (good bike shop and cafés). Continue to the end, then follow the one-way sign and, opposite Coram's Fields, a charity playground which 'adults may only enter if accompanied by a child', turn left into Guildford Street. Take the first right, Lansdowne Terrace, and turn right around the roundabout (Wick Square) into Grenville Street, continuing straight ahead as the street becomes the modernist Brunswick Square, Hunter Street and Judd Street, home to University departments and halls of residence and, at the end, Camden Town Hall.

7 At the junction with busy Euston Road, cross over straight ahead into Midland Road, with St Pancras Station on the right and the new British Library on the left. Continue to the double traffic lights under the railway. Turn right carefully at the first set, and go straight ahead at the second into Goods Way. Take the first left into Camley Street beside the listed Victorian gas holders. Here is Camley Street Natural Park, run by the London Wildlife Trust as 'an oasis for people and wildlife' and well worth a look.

8 Continue under the bridge and along Camley Street for 500m, over the Grand Union Canal (which you aren't allowed to ride – although at publication people were) and turn left just before the next bridge into Barker Drive (environmental area). At the one-way road at the end (St Pancras Way), turn left and carefully cross to take the green stripe right into Georgiana Street. At the road crossing at the end, go over and turn left on the cycle lane signed Somers Town. Follow it down the first right, Pratt Street, and continue through the cycle gap over busy Bayham Street to the main road junction with Camden High Street.

9 Turn right carefully up busy one-way Camden High Street to the junction with Camden Town underground station and continue straight ahead back to Camden Lock.

Camden Lock: great for ethnic wares, grunge clothing and people-watching.

Sunday up the City

S ave this discovery trip around the oldest part of London for Sundays when the offices and markets are shut and the traffic roar dies away. With only the thronging tourists around the Tower of London to contend with, you can follow this winding, compact route in peace, soaking up dozens of sights in an area rich in history and architecture.

Tucked in between the plate-glass behemoths that house the wheeler-dealers of the financial world you'll find quiet mediaeval churchyards and gateways, the modernist Barbican Arts Centre, Little Bangladesh, the site of a famous 1930s street battle when the East End Jews repelled the fascists, the Tower of London and the elegant colonnaded market of Leadenhall with its caviar and champagne stores.

Every inch of the route tells a story, so allow plenty of time to meander. Remember to take sandwiches on a Sunday – the place is as quiet as the graves of the Romans who lie buried in the ground awaiting exhumation by the bulldozers of the next millennium.

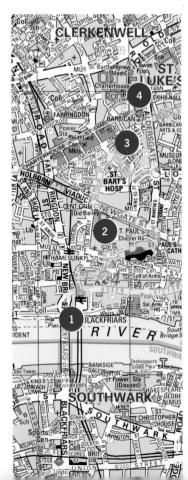

Distance	10km
Grade	Easy – short and flat
Bike	Preferably with smooth tyres
Suitable for children/beginners?	Just about, but the amount of road riding means it's best tackled on a Sunday when the traffic is minimal
Traffic and surface	10 per cent traffic-free, all surfaced, some no-cycling paths
Start and finish	Blackfriars Station
Overground stations	Blackfriars, Cannon Street (closed weekends), City Thameslink (closed weekends), Fenchurch Street, London Bridge, Moorgate, Liverpool Street
Underground stations	Blackfriars, Mansion House, Liverpool Street, Monument, Tower Hill, Whitechapel
Refreshments	Lakeside café at the Barbican, curries in Brick Lane, The Dickens Inn (St Katharine's Dock), fast food at the Tower of London. The pubs and cafés *en route* are mostly shut on Sundays
What to see	St Paul's Cathedral, St Bartholomew's Hospital, Smithfield Market, Barbican Arts Centre, Broadgate Square and Circus and restored Liverpool Street Station, restored Spitalfields Market, Hawksmoor's Christ Church, Spitalfields, Little Bangladesh at Brick Lane, Cable Street, St Katharine's Dock and marina, Tower Bridge, Tower of London, Lloyd's Building, Leadenhall Market, the Monument, Bank of England
What to visit	Tower Bridge, Tower of London, Monument, Bank of England Museum, Barbican Arts Centre

1 Start at the Black Friar pub on the corner of Queen Victoria Street and New Bridge Street outside Blackfriars underground and overground stations. A few metres along Queen Victoria Street, turn left up Black Friars Lane, following the lane for 50m round to the right as it becomes Playhouse Yard, past Printing House Square, where the *London Gazette*, then *The Times* and finally the *Observer* newspapers were produced.

Dismount here, push the bike along Ireland Yard ahead between the barrier, and keep pushing up the second left alley, Burgon Street (where City workers quench their thirsts). The churchyard to the left of Ireland Yard was part of the mediaeval Dominican priory at Blackfriars. At the end of Burgon Street, go straight over and remount to ride up Creed Lane and emerge on to Ludgate Hill, with the view of the west front of St Paul's Cathedral on the right.

2 Take the walkway, St Paul's Churchyard, where you must walk your bike, along the left-hand side of the cathedral to the far end. Where the walkway opens out towards the entrance to St Paul's underground station, turn left into Panyer Alley to the main road, Newgate Street. Turn left carefully on to the main road, then after 100m turn right at the traffic lights into Giltspur Street, signed for St Bartholomew's Hospital. (Old Bailey, the Central Criminal Court, is to the left of the lights. This is the site of Newgate, one of the gates to the City of London, demolished in 1767, and also of Newgate Prison.)

3 At the end of Giltspur Street on West Smithfield Circus, note St Bartholomew's Hospital – better known as Bart's – on your right and the grandiose entrance to Smithfield Market, London's meat market, ahead. Turn to the right and take the cycle path down the alleyway called

Map base © Nicholson 1998

Little Britain. At the end, turn left into Montague Place and left again at the roundabout into Aldersgate Street.

4 After 200m turn right at the lights into Beech Street and continue to the far end of the tunnel. Then turn right into Whitecross Street.

5 This is the entrance to the magnificent Barbican Arts Centre. Use the cycle parking and wander in for a look at the lake, some Shakespeare, a concert or maybe just some refreshments. Then continue riding along Silk Street, turn left into Moor Lane and right into Ropemaker Street. Cross straight over Finsbury Pavement into South Place and continue straight ahead on the cycle lane down Eldon Street.

6 At the end, dismount to the left at the side entrance to Liverpool Street Station. Walk up the marble stairs to the left for a view of Broadgate Circus – a winter-time ice rink. Continue walking ahead around the Circus and through the pedestrian passage to the iron gates. Turn right into Appold

Street, and right at the first lights over the railway bridge along Primrose Street.

7 At the traffic lights at the main road, go straight ahead into Spital Square, and right along the front side of the old Spitalfields market building – a former fruit and veg market currently used for sport, fun fairs, alternative retailing and dining, but now threatened with redevelopment. Turn left at the end along the side of the market, towards Nicholas Hawksmoor's Christ Church, Spitalfields.

At the end, cross Commercial Street and go ahead down the left-hand side of the church along Fournier Street, with its 18th-century terraces now occupied by wealthy city traders. At the end turn left into Brick Lane with its smells, sights and sounds of Little Bangladesh. After the East End Jews moved out to north London, the Bangladeshis moved in. Now the quarter features mosques, sari shops, wonderful curry houses and music.

Take the second right down Hanbury Street, giving way at the change of priority at Spital Street. Continue along Hanbury Street, staying left at the mini-roundabout. Go right to the end and down the alley, turning right onto Vallance Road. Take care crossing Whitechapel Road into New Road, where there is an abrupt architectural change to clothing factories – the rag trade remains the mainstay of the local economy.

8 Continue ahead at the traffic light junction with Commercial Road into Cannon Street Road and continue underneath the railway bridge. Beyond it, turn right into Cable Street, which is commemorated for the 1936 street battle between fascists and local residents, and was bombed to oblivion in the Second World War. Ride along the main carriageway, not the contraflow cycle lane, with the Docklands Light Railway high up on your right for 200m.

Turn left at the lights down Dock Street, signed LCN Wapping. At the junction with The Highway go straight over into Vaughan Way. Turn first right

Left: The timbered gateway leading to the church of St Bartholomew-the-Great. Originally, this was the church doorway, but the nave was demolished in about 1540 during Henry VIII's dissolution of the monasteries.

Opposite: The magnificent west front of St Paul's Cathedral. The route passes to the left.

after 300m at the zebra crossing into Thomas More Street. This is the territory of the Docklands 'yuppy' where derelict docks and wharves have been converted to upmarket housing and marinas. Continue to the end and turn right along the cobbles of St Katharine's Way, with the river through the wasteland to your left, and follow signs to St Katharine's Dock. (For a short diversion on foot to the river front with a view of Tower Bridge, follow the Thames Path signs between the housing.)

9 Explore St Katharine's Dock, the first and most elegant of the resurrected docks, through to the right. Its hostelry is the Dickens Inn.

Continue across the bridge across the dock mouth under the Tower Thistle Hotel, one of the most expensive in the capital. At the end, turn left for the passageway beneath Tower Bridge, where you must walk the bike. (A museum relates the Bridge's history and operation, and you can cross the high-level walkway.) Emerge in front of the Tower of London. Continue to walk the bike and, avoiding the tourists, complete the riverside edge of the Tower, and then turn right up the far side to climb to the main road, Tower Hill.

10 Turn left along Byward Street, dismount and cross right at the pedestrian lights into Great Tower Street and go immediately right up Mark Lane. Note Fenchurch Street Station through to the right. Cross over Fenchurch Street into Billiter Street.

11 At the end turn left into Leadenhall Street and pass the fantastic Lloyd's Building, the work of the architect Richard Rogers, where the plumbing and wiring is elevated to a desirable feature and displayed on the exterior. Continue along Leadenhall Street and turn left down Whittington Avenue into the grand aisles of Leadenhall Market, built in 1881, where the shops retain their period style.

Go straight ahead through the market and turn right at the end into Lime Street. Turn right into Fenchurch Street and left at the lights into Gracechurch Street.

12 Just before the lights, hop on to the pavement and walk the bike to cross at the pedestrian crossing down Fish Street Hill to the

Walk your bike through the tourists outside the Tower of London – or you risk being thrown inside the White Tower.

Monument. This commemorates the start of the Great Fire of London in 1666, which destroyed much of the City of London. Ascend the Monument for a fine view.

Retrace your steps back up Gracechurch Street for 200m to Cornhill on the left. This is officially a no-left turn, so please dismount the bike, walk on the pavement and remount. Continue to the junction, where the Royal Exchange and the Bank of England stand on the right, Mansion House (the Lord Mayor's official residence) on the left. The Bank of England Museum and the Stock Exchange are reached along Threadneedle Street.

To return to the starting-point at Blackfriars, follow Queen Victoria Street ahead and to the left for 800m. Watch the traffic.

Thames Bridges from Chelsea to Lambeth

Cross the Thames three times between Chelsea Harbour and Lambeth on magnificent Victorian bridges between equally splendid embankments. Ride through Battersea Park, beside the Peace Pagoda, and on to the Tate Gallery. Pass the new headquarters of MI6, the secret service, and finish at Lambeth Palace, home of the Archbishop of Canterbury, the religious head of the Church of England, with, across the river, one of the best views of the Palace of Westminster.

On this super ride – one of the best snapshots of London – this book is a little premature. At publication, Sustrans, the sustainable transport charity, is working on the long-term Thames Cycle Route, which should eventually run mostly along the river all the way from Hampton Court in the west, through the centre of the city, to Dartford in the east.

Currently, you can officially ride the route marked in an unbroken line on the map from Chelsea Harbour to Lambeth Bridge via Battersea Park. However, this uses very busy roads and junctions, and is very narrow across Albert Bridge.

Keep an eye open in the future for new pavement cycle paths, marked in dashes on the map. These will eventually get you out of the way of the traffic between Battersea and Chelsea Bridges and along Millbank and Albert Embankment, and provide a diversion along backstreets behind the Tate Gallery.

Also marked in dashes is the natural continuation from the end of our route at Lambeth Bridge along the South Bank to Tower Bridge. These wonderful 4km pass numerous sights on both sides of the river, including the Royal Festival Hall, the National Theatre, the rebuilt Globe Theatre, the Clink Prison museum and Southwark Cathedral. Sustrans tells us that discussions about an official route along this stretch are continuing, and asks that you bear this in mind, go slowly and give way to pedestrians at all times.

1 Park or push the bike, and start with a walkabout around Chelsea Harbour marina, a former canal basin now filled with luxury cruisers and hotels overlooked by Belvedere Tower. Cycling is not allowed inside the automatic car barriers or on the river front.

2 Mount the bike outside the harbour barriers to cross the bridge over Chelsea Creek, where herons can be seen fishing, and take the first right beside the Firkin pub into Lots Road. At the junction at the end, beyond the vast, defunct Lots Road Power Station, turn right into Cheyne Walk, beside Old Wharf and the Chelsea Yacht and Boat Company.

3 Care is needed on this section. Continue for 1km past Battersea Bridge (pavement paths are planned here), and cross the river via Albert Bridge,

built in the early 1870s, taking care on the narrow roadway. On the south side of the Thames, continue down Albert Bridge Road for 200m.

4 Turn left through the ceremonial gates of Battersea Park. Continue straight ahead along the roughly tarmacked North Carriage Drive, past the restored Grand Vista (right), first constructed in 1951 as part of the Festival of Britain. Then comes the Peace Pagoda (left), erected in 1985 and the 70th of its type built around the world by Buddhist monks, and finally the Children's Zoo (right). At the fork go left, and emerge on to Queenstown Road opposite Battersea Power Station (also defunct) and the Adrenalin Village bungee jumping crane.

5 Cross to the other side of Queenstown Road using the toucan crossing and ride carefully over Chelsea Bridge on the pavement.

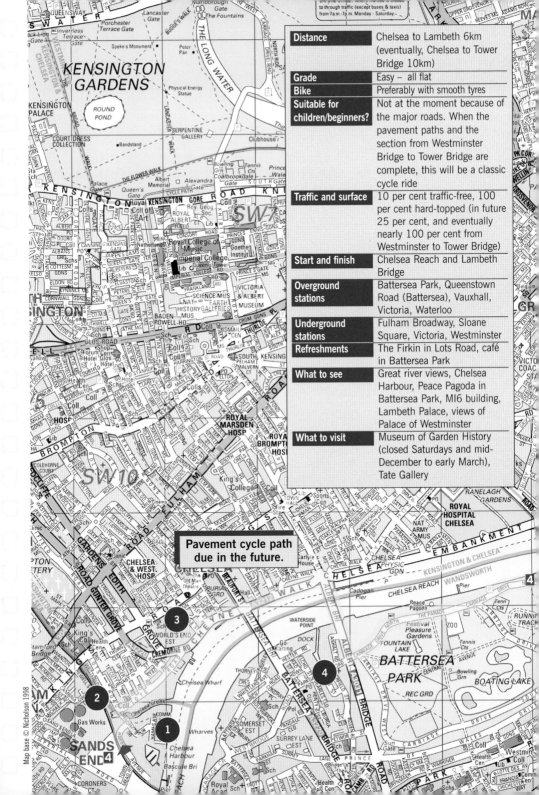

Distance	Chelsea to Lambeth 6km (eventually, Chelsea to Tower Bridge 10km)
Grade	Easy – all flat
Bike	Preferably with smooth tyres
Suitable for children/beginners?	Not at the moment because of the major roads. When the pavement paths and the section from Westminster Bridge to Tower Bridge are complete, this will be a classic cycle ride
Traffic and surface	10 per cent traffic-free, 100 per cent hard-topped (in future 25 per cent, and eventually nearly 100 per cent from Westminster to Tower Bridge)
Start and finish	Chelsea Reach and Lambeth Bridge
Overground stations	Battersea Park, Queenstown Road (Battersea), Vauxhall, Victoria, Waterloo
Underground stations	Fulham Broadway, Sloane Square, Victoria, Westminster
Refreshments	The Firkin in Lots Road, café in Battersea Park
What to see	Great river views, Chelsea Harbour, Peace Pagoda in Battersea Park, MI6 building, Lambeth Palace, views of Palace of Westminster
What to visit	Museum of Garden History (closed Saturdays and mid-December to early March), Tate Gallery

Pavement cycle path due in the future.

ROUTE

4

6 At the far side of the bridge, stay on the pavement, right, into Grosvenor Road. Pass under Grosvenor Bridge and rejoin the road at the pelican crossing opposite Lupus Street.

7 After 1.5km turn right across Vauxhall Bridge to the south bank and the massive Vauxhall Cross junction. Turn left at the traffic lights past the looming new MI6 building along Albert Embankment, and continue along Albert Embankment to Lambeth Bridge. The pavement of Albert Embankment, currently officially out of

bounds, offers magnificent views across the river to the Palace of Westminster. (In the future the pavement along Albert Embankment may be accessible from steps down from Vauxhall Bridge all the way to Westminster Bridge.)

Beyond Lambeth Bridge, on the far side of Lambeth Palace Road is Lambeth Palace, with its handsome Tudor gateway, home to the Archbishop of Canterbury. Next door, the little church of St-Mary-at-Lambeth houses the Garden History Museum; John Tradescant, gardener to Charles I, is buried here.

Tower Bridge along the River to Greenwich

London's maritime history is revealed on this spectacular riverside circuit on both banks of the Thames between Tower Bridge and Greenwich. Start on the north bank, heading through the old villages of Wapping and Limehouse, down the Isle of Dogs, and under the river via the Greenwich foot tunnel. Then return on the south side, through the back streets of old Deptford, past the marinas of Surrey Quays, dipping through old and new Rotherhithe and finishing at the upmarket warehouse housing of Bermondsey.

A good ride for older children, this route has lots to see, including a city farm, a haven of a nature park at Russia Dock, Rotherhithe, and the Design Museum. There are just one or two points where you have to watch the traffic.

Ignore signs saying Thames Path and Riverside Walkway. These tend to be short diversions or dead ends, leading between housing to the riverbank, and are not for cyclists but for walkers. Stick to the route and there'll be plenty to interest you.

Apologies in advance if our directions go out of date since so much building work is going on in Docklands. For a leaflet showing all the Docklands cycle routes, call at the Tourist Information Centre at Canary Wharf, or telephone them on 0171-512 1111; fax: 0171-537 2549.

Distance	15km
Grade	Easy – flat
Bike	Preferably with knobbly tyres
Suitable for children/beginners?	Yes, lots of quiet backstreets and cycle paths and much to see, including the city farm at Surrey Docks. A little traffic awareness is needed at West Ferry Circus and down West Ferry Road
Traffic and surface	20 per cent traffic-free, all surfaced
Start and finish	Tower Bridge
Overground stations	Fenchurch Street, Greenwich, London Bridge
Underground stations	Tower Hill
Refreshments	Dickens Inn (St Katharine's Dock), the Barley Mow pub at Limehouse basin (river terrace), riverfront pubs at Limehouse and Rotherhithe
What to see	Tower Bridge, St Katharine's Dock, Limehouse Basin, mirror-glass Docklands office city, Greenwich Foot Tunnel, Greenwich Market
What to visit	Tower Bridge, National Maritime Museum (including the Old Royal Observatory), Cutty Sark, Gipsy Moth IV, Surrey Docks Farm, Stave Hill Ecology Park, Design Museum

1 Starting from the gravel viewing platform on the north-east side of Tower Bridge, walk past the boy and dolphin statue, across St Katharine's Dock bridge and pick up the brick, then cobbled St Katharine's Way. Continue into Wapping High Street through streets of *nouveau riche* wharf housing, keeping an eye out for the spectacular river views.

2 250m beyond Wapping underground station turn right into Wapping Wall, signposted LCN Limehouse, and continue as far as the bridge over the cut for Shadwell Basin.

3 Immediately after the bridge over the cut, get off your bike and turn right walking down the footpath marked Thames Path beside the tennis courts, opposite Peartree Lane. Push the bike through the riverside King Edward Memorial Park and exit on to the Highway at Free Trade Wharf Square. Turn right and walk along the pavement for about 200m to the entrance to the Limehouse Link tunnel.

At the tunnel entrance turn right into Narrow Street, following the LCN sign to Limehouse and Isle of Dogs. Follow the one-way roads Sport Street and Horseferry Road, rejoining the river at the bridge over the entrance to Limehouse Basin. This is the finishing point of the Grand Union Canal and worth a look around.

4 Continue along Narrow Street through the old hamlet of Limehouse, which has quaint riverfront pubs.

Turn right immediately before the railway bridge at Westferry DLR station, then go right at the lights on to Westferry Road. Continue to the lights, then with care take the central lane up the ramp to Westferry Circus, where you go straight ahead down the far side. Take care rejoining the traffic. At the next roundabout, go straight ahead, not into Marsh Wall, but back into Westferry Road.

(The continuous construction going on in Docklands means that after works on this corner of the river have been completed in 1999, it should again be possible to use the path along the river (marked in dashes on the map) that cuts the corner from Limehouse to Westferry Circus. We guess that directions should then be as follows. Past Limehouse, turn right at the mini-roundabout at Three Colt Street towards the Dundee Wharf development. Turn right at the Enterprise pub and rejoin the riverside on the path along the river. Continue to where the track emerges on to Westferry Road opposite the City Pride pub and turn right, marked LCN Greenwich and Crossharbour.)

5 Continue for 2.5km along the road down to the bottom of the island to Island Gardens station (DLR), passing the *Telegraph* printing works and contrasting private and public housing. At the station, follow the signs for LCN Greenwich to the foot tunnel, built in 1902 and 370 metres long. Take the lift or the stairs and don't cycle in the tunnel.

6 Resurface on the south bank close to the *Cutty Sark* tea clipper and Greenwich village. There are good shops and stalls in and around the market, and the National Maritime Museum is full of nautical exhibits.

(To divert to the Old Royal Observatory at the top of Greenwich Park, pass Cutty Sark, follow the narrow one-way system round the village, and then turn left up Stockwell Street and Nevada Street to enter the Park at the gates. Bizarrely, cycles as well as cars are banned on Avenue Road

Past the old riverside pubs of Limehouse, overlooked by that symbol of ongoing Docklands regeneration, Canary Wharf tower.

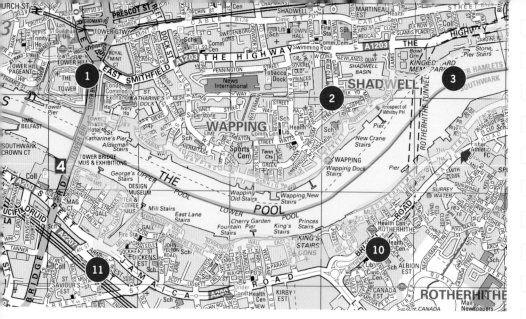

all day on Saturday and Sunday and from 10am to 4pm Mondays to Fridays. Either lock the bike at the bottom or walk it to the Observatory.)

Back on the main route, follow Thames Path signs to the right beside the humbler *Gipsy Moth* yacht (in which Sir Francis Chichester made his circumnavigation) along the streets (walk along one-way Thames Street) that lead to the main Creek Road over Deptford Creek. Turn right and take the first right at the Hoy pub, along Stowage, past St Nicholas Church (ignore the Thames Path sign) and follow the map to Prince Street. At the end turn right into Sayes Court and left behind the shops to Grove Street. Turn right and then right again into Leeway, signposted for Rotherhithe. Follow the map back to the river at Deptford Strand.

7 Stay on the river, which is very grand at this point, for 500m to the entrance to South Dock marina, full of boats and overlooked by the arched Baltic Quay flats.

8 From South Dock, continue in the same direction, and cross the much larger Greenland Dock, which has a cycle path around its perimeter. Follow the cycle signs through Southsea Street, left at Finland Street and immediately right into Bonding Yard Walk.

9 At the end, follow the sign for Surrey Docks Farm and Tower Bridge into Rotherhithe Street.

The farm is worth a visit if you have children with you. Note that the paths to the riverfront are intended for walkers.

From here you can either stay on Rotherhithe Street round the bend in the river, or cut off the corner by exploring the delightful Russia Dock woodlands and Stave Hill Ecology Park, where habitats for birds, insects and plants have been created out of an in-filled dock. At the Mills and Knight Ltd building, take the left turn into Acorn Walk, signposted Bacon's College Ecological Park. Explore on the paths and climb the grassy cone of Stave Hill for a wonderful view, then return either via Beatson Walk or Timber Pond Road to Rotherhithe Street and continue left, westwards.

10 In old Rotherhithe pass to the left of St Mary's Church and take Cottle Way path near the Ship pub. Continue following the signs on the route into Bermondsey, alongside the river at Bermondsey Wall East.

11 Pass the end of Bermondsey Creek and – walking on the pavement – turn right into Shad Thames. Pass the Design Museum before entering the warehouse shops and restaurants of Butler's Wharf that lead back to Tower Bridge. To get to the north side of the river, pass beneath the bridge and take the narrow steps up to the right. The bridge is narrow, so mind the traffic.

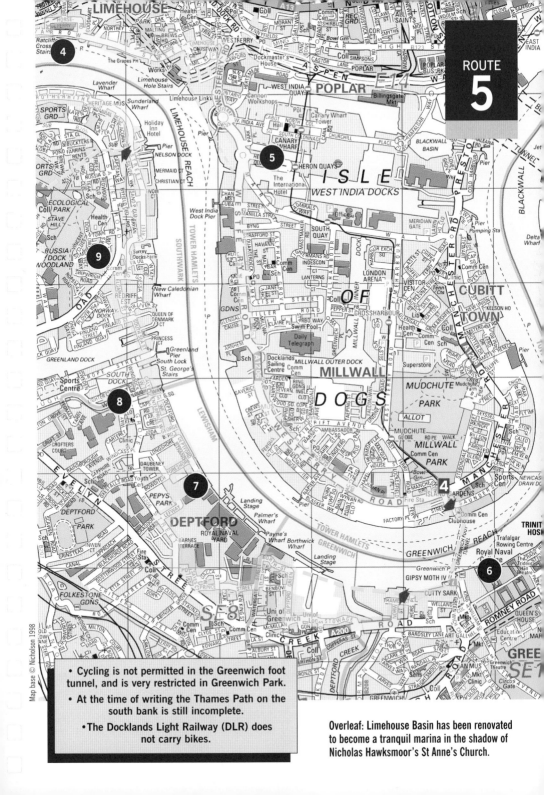

5

- Cycling is not permitted in the Greenwich foot
  tunnel, and is very restricted in Greenwich Park.
- At the time of writing the Thames Path on the
  south bank is still incomplete.
- The Docklands Light Railway (DLR) does
  not carry bikes.

Overleaf: Limehouse Basin has been renovated
to become a tranquil marina in the shadow of
Nicholas Hawksmoor's St Anne's Church.

Map base © Nicholson 1998

The Isle of Dogs

Wealth, poverty and maritime history cohabit in riveting proximity on this short, spectacular road ride around the heart of London's recycled docks. The route runs across the toes of 50-storey Canary Wharf Tower (visible from so many other routes) and rubs shoulders with offices wrecked by the massive 1996 IRA bomb. Shabby post-modernist council estates share streets with chintzy private housing, while, oblivious to the upheaval, Sir Christopher Wren's Royal Naval College gazes implacably across the river from Greenwich. Here the Thames bears the first signs of the mighty estuary it is to become.

Distance	7km
Grade	Easy – short and flat
Bike	Preferably with smooth tyres
Suitable for children/beginners?	Yes, with a little care at road junctions. The roads are quieter at weekends
Traffic and surface	5 per cent traffic-free, all surfaced
Start and finish	Island Gardens
Overground stations	Greenwich
Refreshments	Canary Wharf, ASDA restaurant, City Pride pub
What to see	The Thames, Canary Wharf Tower, views across to Greenwich
What to visit	Mudchute City Farm

1 From the north-bank entrance of Greenwich Foot Tunnel, turn right on to Saunders Ness Road. (The signposted River Walk leads to the riverside, but should not be cycled.) Ride to the end and turn left into Seyssel Street, just before the private estate starts, to get to the main road.

2 Turn right on to Manchester Road. (The entrance to Mudchute City Farm is opposite.) Continue for 2km using the cycle paths. Follow the cycle path on to the pavement just before the major roundabout with the A1261.

3 Pick up the cycle track that leads left and westwards up Trafalgar Way towards the tower, signposted Canary Wharf. (Don't turn down the subway signed Poplar.) Security has been tightened since the IRA bombed the island but you

should pass without problem through a cordon at Cartier Circle.

4 Pass the foot of the tower itself, officially called 1 Canada Square, and explore the buildings and docksides of Cabot Square on foot if you wish. There is plenty of cycle parking around and in the underground car parks. Then continue straight ahead westwards out of the buildings to Westferry Circus roundabout.

5 Until 1999 building works block the riverside path, so you must turn left down the ramp off the Circus, join the road below and continue to the next roundabout. Here take the second left into Marsh Wall.

(From 1999 you should be able to dismount on the far side of Westferry Circus and carry the bike down the wide flight of granite steps to the magnificent riverside. Then turn left at the bottom and follow the track to its end at Westferry Road. Cross the road and pass by the side of the City Pride pub seen ahead to turn right on to Marsh Wall.)

After 500m turn right under South Quay station into Millharbour.

6 Just before the end of Millharbour, turn left at the LCN sign Crossharbour through Pepper Street Arcade, cross Glengall Bridge and immediately turn right beside the circular brick building to get on to Turnberry Quay. Continue along the dock for 200m and go left behind the large grass dais, to return under the railway to the road up the ramp.

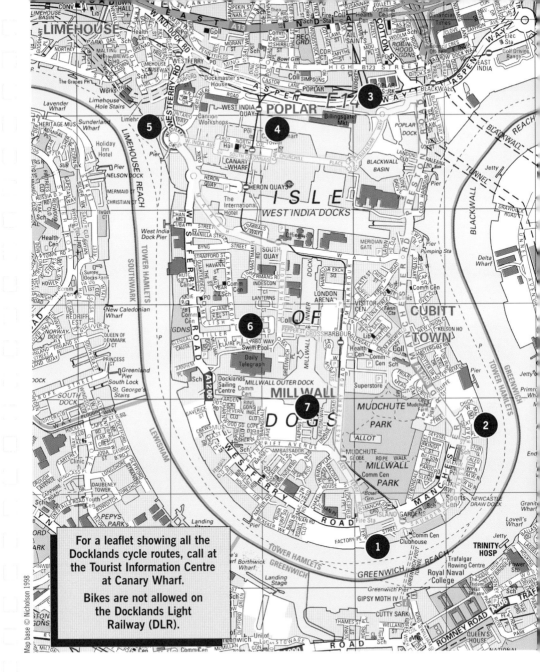

For a leaflet showing all the Docklands cycle routes, call at the Tourist Information Centre at Canary Wharf.

Bikes are not allowed on the Docklands Light Railway (DLR).

7 Turn right down East Ferry Road for 1km back to Westferry Road. Turn left on to Manchester Road again, to complete the circuit at Island Gardens DLR station ahead.

Overleaf: The view along Millwall Inner dock to Canary Wharf and the Docklands Light Railway.

Greenway and the Royal Docks

This ride is more than a tour of monuments to East London's industrial history – it is also green, atmospheric and substantially car-free. We start with the glories of Victorian sanitation, turn around the vast, defunct Royal Docks, touch the shining Thames Barrier and towering Canary Wharf, and finish at House Mill, an 18th-century Dutch-style gin mill. There is a big renewal programme around Royal Docks, including London City Airport and much new housing.

The first 6km follow the Greenway, a regenerated pathway that runs from Bow to East Ham along the embankment of the Northern Outfall Sewer, a great 1860s engineering project that relieved the polluted Thames. Apart from the occasional background whiffiness, you never know what you are riding on!

At Greenway's end, the route turns back into the new Beckton estate and taps into the growing network of Docklands cycle routes to reach the spectacular expanse of the Royal Docks. Further on you see the sugar refineries and breweries that depend on the river for water. Into the concrete jungle of the Isle of Dogs, up pops a new bird sanctuary and a view of the great kink in the Thames. Then the route turns north through the backstreets of Poplar to finish at Three Mills, the oldest collection of buildings in the Lee Valley waterway system.

Distance	16km
Grade	Medium – flat, but a distance
Bike	Preferably with smooth tyres
Suitable for children/beginners?	Yes, because there is so much traffic-free riding. But it's a long way for little legs and North Woolwich Road is busy, although less so at the weekends
Traffic and surface	50 per cent traffic-free, all surfaced
Start and finish	Entrance to the Greenway, 750m east of Bow flyover on Stratford High Street E15 (the A11)
Overground stations	Silvertown & City Airport, Stratford, West Ham
Underground stations	Bromley-by-Bow, West Ham, Plaistow
Refreshments	ASDA at Beckton, Canary Wharf (off-route) during shopping hours
What to see	Abbey Mills pumping station, Royal Docks, Thames Barrier, Lyle Park, East India Dock bird sanctuary, Isle of Dogs skyline, Three Mills
What to visit	Three Mills (open Sunday afternoons, March to October – for information on events telephone 0181-215 0050/0051)

1 Pick up the Greenway on the south side of Stratford High Street, E15, 750m east of the Bow flyover and follow it in more or less a straight line for 6km to the end at East Ham. Crossing numerous roads, the path runs through the light industry and waterway system of the Lee Valley, past the ornate Abbey Mills sewage station at Mill Meads (built by Sir Joseph Bazalgette, the Victorian engineering master) and the East London cemetery, through Plaistow, eventually emerging opposite East Ham nature reserve, created in another small cemetery. Turn right into High Street South to the immediate junction with the A13 Newham Way. (The sewer continues to the works on the Thames.)

2 Go straight ahead at the lights along A117 Woolwich Manor Way, past the Beckton Alp ski centre on your left (where a mountain bike downhill course is planned), and straight ahead at the roundabout to pick up the cycle route, the Coke Route or Beckton Corridor, between the houses on the right beside the shopping centre and opposite Beckton DLR station. (There is a café in ASDA.)

After 1.5km between the houses and parkland, at the paved circle follow the sign left for Silvertown (also Royal Albert DLR station). Over the brow of the path, the expanse of Royal Albert Dock comes into view. Proceed beneath the DLR to the dockside, and then turn right to take the spiral Connaught

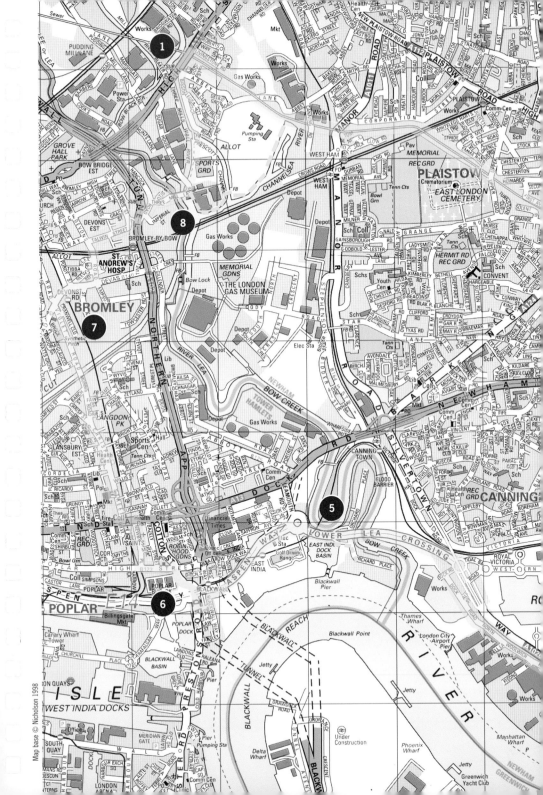

ROUTE

7

The Greenway is locked after dark.

Bikes are not allowed on the Docklands Light Railway (DLR).

For information on cycling and sites of historic interest in the Lee Valley Park, telephone the Lee Valley Regional Park Authority on 01992 702200; fax: 01992 702230.

For a leaflet showing all the Docklands cycle routes, visit the Tourist Information Centre at Canary Wharf; tel: 0171-512 1111; fax: 0171-537 2549.

Map base © Nicholson 1998

Footbridge to the south side of the dock. To the west is Royal Victoria Dock.

3 On the far side of the bridge, pass underneath main Connaught Bridge (A1020) above and take the road on the right to the mini-roundabout. Take the third exit, right. At the big roundabout after a few metres (watch for the Tate & Lyle sugar refinery tankers), take the first exit, left, marked the Blackwall Tunnel. At the third roundabout (North Woolwich roundabout) go right to pick up the cycle route west along North Woolwich Road.

(After 200m on the left is the entrance to the Thames Barrier, which is worth a diversion through the wasteland approach, where a new park is under construction. Unfortunately, the visitor centre is located on the south bank.)

Another very pleasant diversion is Lyle Park further along North Woolwich Road. 1km on from the Barrier, turn left into Bradfield Road for the park entrance on the left. The tranquil park between the industrial sites was donated to the Borough of West Ham by the sugar refiners in 1912 and occupies a precious 50m of riverfront, however, there is no cycling in the park.

4 250m further along North Woolwich Road, take Dock Road, the side road to the left of the flyover, and continue past the old Tate & Lyle refinery and the Charrington brewery to the end. Follow the cycle signs. At the roundabout stay on the cycle path along Lower Lea Crossing, pass the timber yards and nature reserves of Bow Creek, which twists and turns as it escapes to Old Father Thames. Watch for herons.

On the far side of the Creek, turn left back on yourself down the slope into Orchard Place and divert right at the bottom round to the East India Dock bird sanctuary.

5 Return to the cycle path on the main road and continue westwards. At the roundabout continue westwards on the path (signed LCN Isle of Dogs/Greenwich, not City) beside the fast road (Aspen Way). Pass the Reuters building (satellite dish on top), designed by Richard Rogers. Stay with the path as it moves into back streets and emerge at the traffic light T-junction with Preston's Road.

6 Use the Toucan lights to cross Preston's Road to the shared cycle/footway on the far side, go right

and head down the cycle track subway that leads under the roundabout. Follow signs for Poplar back up to Preston's Road, turn right briefly and take the first left into Poplar High Street, signed LCN City and Hackney.

Take the second right, Newby Place, past Hawksmoor's All Saints Church to reach busy East India Dock Road. Cross over using the pedestrian crossing on the left and go north up Chrisp Street ahead. Pass Chrisp Street market on your left and converted Spratts warehousing/housing on your right, cross Limehouse Cut (now permanently closed to bikes, as it is too narrow and floods), and continue as the road becomes Morris Road and Violet Road to the mini-roundabout with Devons Road at the end.

7 Turn right into Devons Road at the mini-roundabout, and go straight on at the next one, past the DLR station. Over the bridge, take the second left (still Devons Road) and the first right after the low bridge, Talwin Street. At the end on the left-hand bend, walk the bike on to the dual-carriageway pavement round to the left, and find the subway that leads under the motorway to Tesco. Emerge at the supermarket, walk the bike in front of it, and turn right down Three Mill Lane.

8 Ride down to the old mills. In House Mill on the left, built in the Dutch style in 1776, grain was ground for distilling gin. Turn left through the buildings, pick up the towpath beside the river and follow it back to the main road (A11 High Street). The entrance to Greenway is 100m to the right.

If you want to cut off the ride's top corner, take the Long Wall Path from Three Mills past Abbey Mills pumping station to the Greenway. Please take particular care on the first section and crossing the Prescott Channel bridge, where it is better to dismount altogether.

Right: Signing on the Greenway

Overleaf: Clock Mill on Three Mills Island – a gem hidden amid east London's light industry.

Marshes and Meadows of the Lee Valley

Here's a sweet turn around the canals, marshes and meadows of Hackney and Walthamstow, and nearly all off-road into the bargain. Note that you can only complete the full circuit after a dry spell – on Walthamstow Marshes near Coppermill Lane there is a section beneath low railway lines that gets flooded and completely impassable after wet weather, particularly in winter. Also note that up the quiet backwater of the River Lee above Old Ford the path is narrow and a bit creepy, so take care here and don't ride alone.

We start at Old Ford Locks, run up the River Lee beside Hackney Marsh, past the Middlesex Filter Beds nature reserve and then alongside Walthamstow Marsh nature reserve (please stick to the path), to return down the towpath of the Lee Navigation to Old Ford.

Although they are cyclable, two sections are in need of work. These are the backwater mentioned above between Old Ford and Carpenters Road and the stretch under the railway lines on Walthamstow Marshes where you have to duck your head! These two sections form part of the Lee Valley pathway, a 25-mile route all the way from Ware, Hertfordshire, south to Greenwich on the Thames, due for completion around the year 2000. The track, which is route number one in the National Cycle Network developed by Sustrans, is designed to relieve cycle congestion on the River Lea/Lee Navigation towpath. For an information leaflet on the Pathway, contact Lee Valley Park Information Centre, Abbey Gardens, Waltham Abbey, Essex EN9 1XQ; tel: 01992 702200; fax: 01992 702230.

Distance	13km
Grade	Easy – flat, but narrow canalside in one place and a very low bridge in another
Bike	Preferably with knobbly tyres
Suitable for children/beginners?	Yes. Lots of traffic-free riding and open space
Traffic and surface	90 per cent traffic-free, all surfaced
Start and finish	Old Ford Locks
Overground stations	Clapton, Hackney Wick, Stratford
Refreshments	Prince of Wales pub on Lea Bridge Road
What to see	Old Ford Locks and *Big Breakfast* studios, Middlesex Filter Beds nature reserve, Walthamstow Marsh nature reserve, Springfield Marina

The green corridor of the Lee Valley, used by migrating birds and cyclists alike.

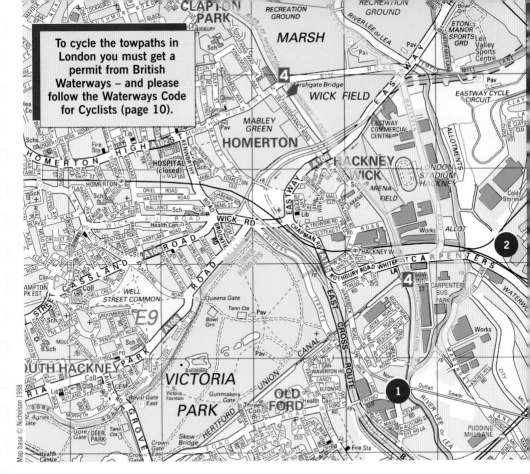

To cycle the towpaths in London you must get a permit from British Waterways – and please follow the Waterways Code for Cyclists (page 10).

1 Find picturesque Old Ford Locks – home to TV's *The Big Breakfast* – at the end of Dace Road. Cross the black and white bridge and follow the sign for Carpenters Road left up the river path (not up the canal). Ignore the waterways leading off to the right. Cross over the green bridge and go left carefully where the track narrows. Cross the black and white bridge to the high-level path and continue to Carpenter's Road.

2 Turn left into Carpenter's Road and take the first right up Waterden Road, through the industrial sites past Hackney Dog Stadium. At the lights go straight ahead and pick up the path on the right beside the River Lea, just on the other side of Homerton Road.

3 Continue to the railings of the Middlesex Filter Beds, now a nature reserve open to the public

during the summer (call Lee Valley Information on 01992 702200 for opening times). Follow its perimeter around to pick up the towpath of the Lee Navigation northwards. (When the Lee Valley Pathway is complete it will cross the river via a new bridge linking Hackney Marsh and Walthamstow Marsh via Essex Filter beds, making this route a true circuit rather than a figure of eight.)

4 Leave the towpath through the car park of the Princes of Wales pub, turn right eastwards, on to Lea Bridge Road. (Walk the bike along the pavement if you prefer to keep out of the way of the heavy traffic.)

5 Pass the Lee Valley Ice Centre, then after 100m turn left northwards away from the road, following the sign for St James Street, Walthamstow, Chingford, along the gravelled track, past the

55

Lea Bridge Riding School. Continue along this filled-in aqueduct to the crossing of railway lines.

6 Here you hit a short piece of track due for upgrading soon as part of the Lee Valley Pathway. This side of the arches, leave the track, go right and duck carefully under the very low railway line - mind your head! In winter the path here is usually flooded and completely impassable. Turn left and go through the neighbouring arches to continue northwards over the grass banking, with the fenced-in Thames Water Coppermills Water Treatment Works on the right. Continue in the same direction across the field to the far corner and emerge through the gate on to Coppermill Lane. Turn left under the railway.

7 Continue across the top edge of Walthamstow Marsh Nature Reserve, a Site of Special Scientific Interest (SSSI), to Springfield Marina,

then turn left through the bike gates and get back on to the towpath of the canal beside the narrow boats.

8 Continue southwards for about 1.5km (to just before the steely-green ice rink) and go right over the black and white footbridge to the far side of the canal. Stay heading south on the towpath under the Lea Bridge Road past the pub. Continue along the canal for 4km back to Old Ford Locks, following the signs for alternative parallel tracks where you are not allowed on the towpath itself.

Right: The green corridor of the Lee Valley, used by migrating birds and cyclists alike. Walthamstow marsh is a nature reserve of atmospheric beauty bordered by the Lee Navigation.

Overleaf: Idyll in E5 – pootling along the Lee Navigation.

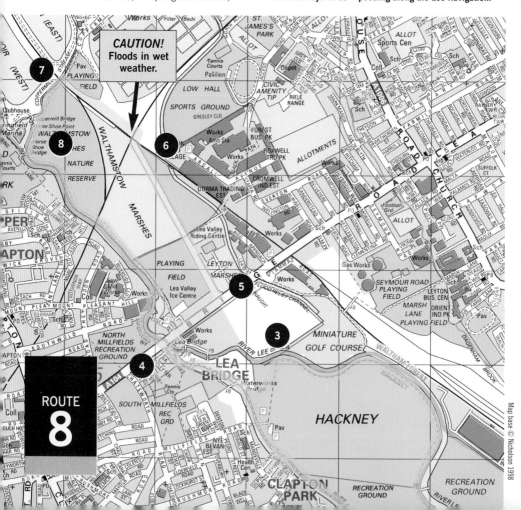

ROUTE 8

Map base © Nicholson 1998

Green Tour d'Hackney

The hustle and bustle of Hackney is relieved by several open spaces, four of them touched on this tour. Tracks across Hackney Downs, South and North Mill Fields, London Fields, Victoria Park (laid out in 1842 and the oldest municipal park in the world) and the towpaths of the Regent's and Hertford Union Canals together account for 5km of car-free riding out of 10km – not bad for one of the most densely populated areas in London. The road sections include several nasty right-hand turns, particularly at the junctions of Chatsworth Road/Millfields Road, Lower Clapton Road/Downs Road, and Downs Road/Cricketfield Road, where you must either ride with great care or dismount altogether. These hairy crossings spoil what is otherwise a highly suitable ride for children and beginners.

Distance	10km
Grade	Easy – flat and short
Bike	Preferably with knobbly tyres
Suitable for children/beginners?	Yes, but there are half-a-dozen right-hand turns on the road where you must take care
Traffic and surface	50 per cent traffic-free; all surfaced, rough in places
Start and finish	Cycle route at Falcon and Firkin pub on Victoria Park Road
Overground stations	Clapton, Hackney Central, Hackney Downs, Hackney Wick, Homerton, London Fields
Underground stations	Bow Road and Mile End
Refreshments	Falcon and Firkin pub (Victoria Park), jellied eels (Broadway Market), the Dove (Broadway Market), the Prince of Wales (Lea Bridge Road)
What to see	Cycle strip across South Mill Fields, the old churchyard at Churchwell Path, canals and jellied eels

1 At the Falcon and Firkin pub on the northern edge of Victoria Park on Victoria Park Road, cross at the cycle lights on to the green-strip cycle track along Gascoyne Road. Stay on the green strip all the way to the end, down Kenton Road, and follow the arrow left into Valentine Road. Just after

Tesco's, which you keep on your left, take Milborne Street, a little passage on your right between the chip shop and TV dealer.

Turn right at the end of Milborne Street into Elsdale Street, and follow the road round to the right, becoming Chatham Place. At the end, cross Morning Lane, at the zebra if you wish, and continue straight ahead along the passage under the railway, Churchwell Path. Follow this along the churchyard to its end at Lower Clapton Road. Cross, continue straight ahead into Clapton Square, and turn right at the end, Clapton Passage. Cross over and continue straight ahead into Powerscroft Road, forking left half way along.

2 At the bottom, either cross over at the zebra or ride left along Chatsworth Road briefly, to turn right on to the green cycle strip across the lawns of South Mill Fields. Continue for 500m to the far corner for a brief foray on the canal. Turn left on to the towpath and stay on it under the bridge, to the right of the Prince of Wales pub. Beyond the bridge, turn immediately left up the granite ramp and continue along the track through North Millfields, parallel to Lea Bridge Road.

At the lights, it's straight over back into Chatsworth Road and back to the corner where you joined South Mill Fields. Now turn right, with care, up Millfields Road for a bit of a climb. Just before the end at the railed gardens, turn right into little Lower Clapton Road, and left again to reach the main Lower Clapton Road. At the lights there, turn right with care into Downs Road. After 100m turn right, taking great care, to stay on Downs Road for

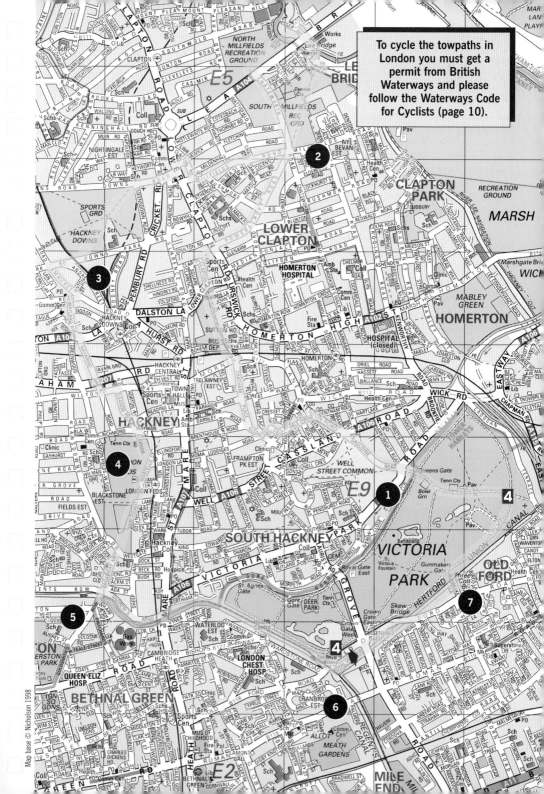

To cycle the towpaths in London you must get a permit from British Waterways and please follow the Waterways Code for Cyclists (page 10).

another 100m. At the Downs, take the track diagonally across the grass, straight over a concrete circle, to the far corner to leave on Downs Park Road.

3 Turn right, then left on to the main Amhurst Road. Soon, at the mini-roundabout, turn right into Sandringham Road and immediately left into Wayland Avenue. Continue straight ahead at Dalston Lane on to the cycle path of Navarino Road. Cross over main Graham Road, and take the first left into Wilton Way, and then the first right into Eleanor Road. Cross Richmond Road at the end and pick up the track through London Fields.

4 At the end, at the Pub on the Park, turn right into Martello Street, past the pub, and then turn right on the cycle path back on to the Fields. Continue to the end, the cycle path crossing over Lansdowne Drive and into Broadway Market.

5 At the end, find the gate to the Regent's Canal towpath in Regent's Row to the right. Turn left on the canal and continue for 1.5km. It's narrow in places and there are lots of anglers to give way to.

6 Where the towpath rises over the canal junction, turn left up the Hertford Union Canal, built in 1830 to link the Regent's Canal and River Lee Navigation. Continue for 1km to the third bridge, Three Colts Bridge, which bears a heritage trail sign and carries Gunmaker's Lane over. Here leave the canal, turning left into Victoria Park.

7 Turn right inside the park and follow the wide designated cycle track along the outside edge, to the end, St Mark's Gate. Turn left across the park, back to the Falcon and Firkin.

Right: London Fields after a rain shower.

Below: East End life is alive and wriggling in Broadway Market.

Hampstead Heath and Parkland Walk

Hampstead Heath may be renowned for poets, kites and drinking holes, but it won't go down in history for its cycle tracks. Considering its size, cyclists get a strictly limited share of the pie. The three linear tracks you are permitted to ride finish at roads, which means a circular tour within the Heath doesn't exist.

This ride is split into long and short loops. Our long route down to Finsbury Park makes the best of a bad job. Although a third of the riding is car-free, the rest is on-road and much of it very busy, so we cannot recommend this route for children. The short loop keeps to the Heath as far as possible.

From Hampstead Heath station, the route scrambles over the Heath, passes two famous pubs, Jack Straw's Castle and the Spaniards, and then heads for the smart hill village of Highgate. Here the short loop turns down across the Heath again.

The long circuit continues 3km to Finsbury Park down Parkland Walk, an old railway line. From there, it follows a web of cycle paths, backroads and parks to get back to the Heath. It isn't ideal, but it closes the circle as pleasantly as possible.

Bike muggings have taken place on Parkland Walk, so be sensible and don't ride it alone or after dark. Please also ride considerately of pedestrians.

Distance	Short loop 9km; long loop 17km
Grade	Medium – hilly
Bike	Preferably with knobbly tyres
Suitable for children/beginners?	Unfortunately no. The cycle path across the Heath spits you out at a very busy junction, and most of the roads are fast and furious
Traffic and surface	35 per cent traffic-free; 30 per cent natural, 70 per cent hard-top
Start and finish	Hampstead Heath station
Overground stations	Crouch Hill, Finsbury Park, Gospel Oak, Hampstead Heath, Finsbury Park, Upper Holloway. Crouch Hill, Gospel Oak and Upper Holloway are on the Rolling Cycleway
Refreshments	Spaniards Inn (Spaniards Road), Jack Straw's Castle (Whitestone Pond), the Flask (Highgate village), Kenwood House café (Hampstead Lane), Hampstead and Highgate villages, Jacksons Lane Arts Centre, Highgate
What to see	Hampstead mixed bathing pond, sculptures on Parkland Walk
What to visit	Kenwood House, with its art gallery

1 Turn right out of the station and climb up the main South End Road for 100m (ignore the tree-lined path on your right) to the Heath car park.

2 Here, pick up the cycle track (8mph speed limit, marked by yellow cycles) and follow it as it passes between the ponds (the mixed bathing pond is on the left). Continue as the track turns leftwards and climbs for 1.5km to emerge at the top of the Heath on to busy Spaniards Road.

3 Leaving the Heath, briefly turn left, watching the busy junction outside Jack Straw's Castle pub – dismount if you prefer. Then turn right down the right-hand northern edge of Whitestone Pond, and go right again down West Heath Road. Descend on the road down the zig-zags for 800m.

4 Watch out on the right for the wide track, Sandy Road, on to West Heath. Follow this for 500m past Leg of Mutton pond. The animal pens of Golders Hill Park children's zoo are on your left.

5 Emerge through the houses opposite the Bull and Bush pub, and – watch the busy traffic – turn right carefully on to the road for a stiff climb

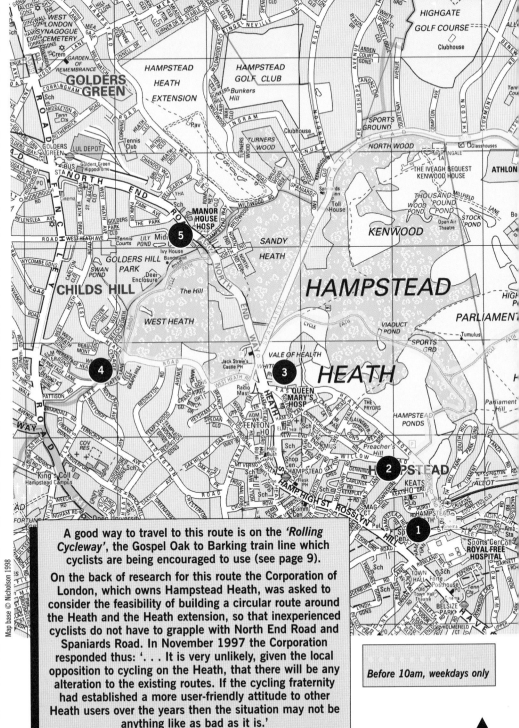

A good way to travel to this route is on the *'Rolling Cycleway'*, the Gospel Oak to Barking train line which cyclists are being encouraged to use (see page 9).

On the back of research for this route the Corporation of London, which owns Hampstead Heath, was asked to consider the feasibility of building a circular route around the Heath and the Heath extension, so that inexperienced cyclists do not have to grapple with North End Road and Spaniards Road. In November 1997 the Corporation responded thus: '. . . It is very unlikely, given the local opposition to cycling on the Heath, that there will be any alteration to the existing routes. If the cycling fraternity had established a more user-friendly attitude to other Heath users over the years then the situation may not be anything like as bad as it is.'

Before 10am, weekdays only

Map base © Nicholson 1998

back up to Jack Straw's Castle. Turn left here along Spaniards Road, minding the traffic (cyclists aren't allowed to use the track on the left, the law requiring that you be squeezed by cars driving at 40mph instead), and through the old toll gate at the Spaniards pub. (The entrance to Kenwood House is on the right soon after. It is well worth a diversion here to look at the superb paintings and enjoy the smashing café.) Continue along Hampstead Lane, for a total of 2.5km, up to Highgate village.

6 Short loop: Just before Hampstead Lane finishes at the mini-roundabout at Highgate, take the last right turn into The Grove, then the first right into Fitzroy Park. Follow this pleasant road steeply downwards and curving left, becoming Millfield Road. Continue straight ahead where it comes alongside the Heath.

Ignore the first track right across the Heath, and take the second track, clearly signed Cycleway, between the ponds. Continue on this track straight ahead, following the markings (speed limit 8mph).

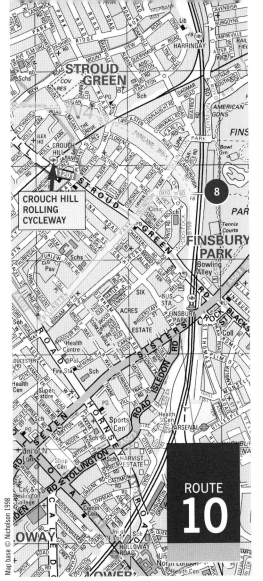

CROUCH HILL ROLLING CYCLEWAY

ROUTE 10

Community Centre at the lights has a cool café.) At the traffic lights with Archway Road, turn right and almost immediately first left into Holmesdale Road.

7 After 20m, the entrance to Parkland Walk is found at the five-bar gate. Continue as the former railway track drops down a gentle grade for 3km, through old platforms and past sculptures. Please ride carefully and give priority to pedestrians – Haringey Council has received complaints about 'intimidatory' cyclists.

8 Nearing Finsbury Park, you come to a bridge going left over the main railway line. (For Finsbury Park station, cross the bridge, turn right, and continue for another 300m to the end of the path.) Turn right down the slope into Oxford Road, then turn left on to Tollington Park Road. Go straight ahead at the lights into Tollington Park. At the end, turn right into Hornsey Road, and after 400m left into Marlborough Road. At the kink after 400m, turn left into Kiver Road, then immediately right into Davenant Road, and emerge at Holloway Road.

Cross Holloway Road at the cycle lights and continue straight ahead through Whittington Park on the cycle path. Turn right back on to the road at the end, and continue around the corner, becoming Foxham Road. At the end of the straight section, go through the gated railings on the right and cross the playing field. Emerge beside the entrance to student halls. Turn right and then immediately left into Station Road. At the end, turn right briefly into Junction Road and immediately left into Wyndham Crescent. At the end, turn right briefly up Dartmouth Park and immediately left into Chetwynd Road. At the end, turn right at the traffic lights.

9 After 400m take the entrance on the left back on to Hampstead Heath along the metalled road by the tennis courts. Continue straight ahead, past the staff offices and café, for 750m.

Passing the athletics track, turn left by the brick pavilion over the railway lines, then right into Savernake Road and Constantine Road. You will have to walk along the pavement to the cluster of shops at the station, as the roads are one-way – an unfortunate damp-squib end to the ride. However, if you happen to have reached here before 10am on weekday mornings, you can continue straight ahead at the brick pavilion and leave the Heath by Nassington Road, turning left into Parliament Hill and left again into South Hill Park.

After a few hundred metres, at a junction with a choice of cycleways, take the left fork and follow the markings to retrace your steps back past the mixed bathing pond and onwards to East Heath Road. The station is leftwards down the road.

Long loop: At the end of Hampstead Lane, turn left at the mini-roundabout, then after 100m turn right carefully on to a busy road and after 50m left into Southwood Lane. After 100m turn right, down through the width restriction of Jacksons Lane. (Jacksons Lane Arts and

Barnet Brookside

C ontrast frenetic concrete jungle with timeless green-belt ridges and old villages in this pleasant tour of the Barnet's green spaces. From an ugly but well-engineered start at Brent Cross shopping centre on the North Circular Road, the route tracks the course of Dollis Brook northwards along quiet streets and green parkland on a set of enlightened cycle routes. Below Barnet town we turn back to close the circle via Totteridge, the Mill Hill Ridgeway and through old and new Hendon, once again on cycle paths. When the research was done, not all the routes had been installed, but they were due for completion soon.

According to Barnet Council, footpaths in Totteridge Vale, around which most of the route revolves, are unlikely ever to be turned into bridleways. This would allow cyclists to enjoy the valley off-road and avoid the nasty road along Totteridge Common. Apparently, the local Totteridge Manor Association is totally opposed to bridleways.

Distance	27km
Grade	Medium – some hills
Bike	Preferably with knobbly tyres
Suitable for children/beginners?	The traffic is tight at Brent Cross shopping centre, and Barnet Lane and Totteridge Common are narrow with fast driving, spoiling what is otherwise a quiet green route with long parkland sections
Traffic and surface	6km car-free riding, rough in places
Start and finish	Staples Corner near Brent Cross, or to suit
Overground stations	Cricklewood, Hendon
Underground stations	You can take a bike along these sections of the Northern Line only: East Finchley to High Barnet, Golders Green to Hendon Central
Refreshments	Greyhound (Hendon), Rising Sun (Highwood Hill), Orange Tree (Totteridge) and Hammers (Mill Hill Ridgeway)
What to see	Grasslands beside Dollis Brook, Totteridge and Mill Hill villages, footbridge view of junction 2 of the M1, old Hendon with St Mary's Church
What to visit	Church Farm Museum, Hendon

1 Pick up the signed cycle route beneath the flyover on the southern side of Staples Corner roundabout (junction of the North Circular Road and the Edgware Road) where it crosses the southern slip road. Follow the signs for 1km, initially along Tilling Road. At a roundabout, the cycle path turns right on to Templehof Avenue, back on itself and then across the North Circular Road to Brent Cross shopping centre.

The signs peter out here, so turn right at the roundabout to the west of the building, ride along Prince Charles Drive in front of it, and at the busy traffic lights at the far end carefully take the right fork. (There is a car-free track through the fence on the right that leads down under the flyover, but it is difficult to cross to, so stay on the road.) Take care through the subway, and emerge at a roundabout.

2 Take the second exit into Shirehall Lane and continue in this direction for 1.5km, along Green Lane and Alexandra Road as far the T-junction with Finchley Lane. Turn right carefully, drop to the lights (over Dollis Brook) and take the first left into Broughton Avenue. Ignore the cycle signs that turn you left down Waverley Grove.

3 Continue across along Broughton Avenue and, where the tarmac ends, pick up the park track for the start of 1km of pleasant parkland. This is full of children, dogs and people, so ride watchfully and considerately.

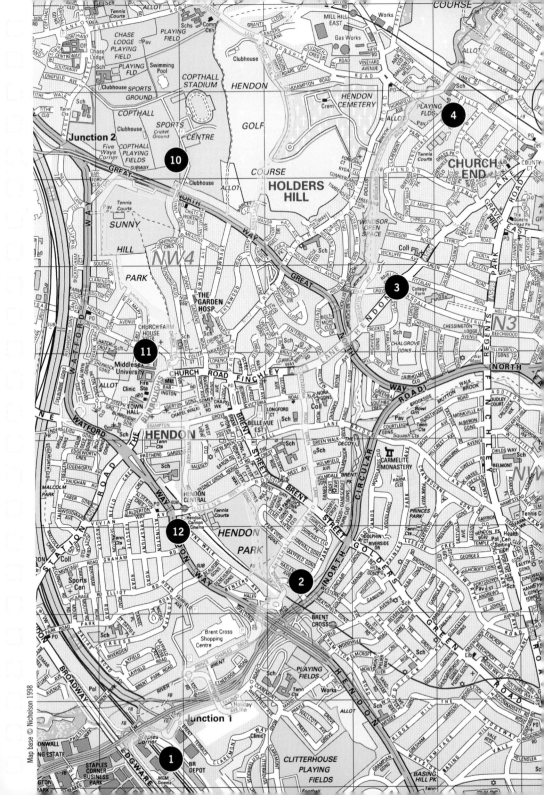

4 After 1km, leave the park at the end over a footbridge, turn right carefully on to the road (signed Whetstone) and continue for 200m. Beyond the high arches, take the first left into Gordon Road and continue in the same direction for 2.5km, along Brent Way, Chesterfield Road, Westbury Road and Holden Road. Then, 500m beyond Woodside Park underground station, turn left down Laurel View.

5 After 100m turn right for another shot of sweet, green parkland. Continue for 1km to Totteridge Lane. Turn right and climb the hill briefly to pick up the track on the far side below Totteridge underground station, and continue in the same direction for 1.5km to Barnet.

6 At King George V playing fields, leave the brookside, pass the black and white barrier and climb the right-hand side of the playing fields. Turn out of the park into Grasvenor Avenue. Continue uphill, turning left into Fairfield Way, then left into Westcombe Drive, past Barnet FC ground. At the end, turn left into Barnet Lane. (Eventually the parkland track should continue through King George V Playing Fields, cutting out this detour.)

7 Climb on narrow, cycle-unfriendly Barnet Lane for 1.5km to the war memorial junction at Totteridge village. St Andrew's parish church is just to the left and the Orange Tree pub lies 200m along the road to the left. Turn right and follow the road for 3km along picturesque Totteridge Common, unfortunately enlivened by Damon Hill wannabes on the twists and turns. There isn't even the relief of a track along the swards as an alternative!

ROUTE
11

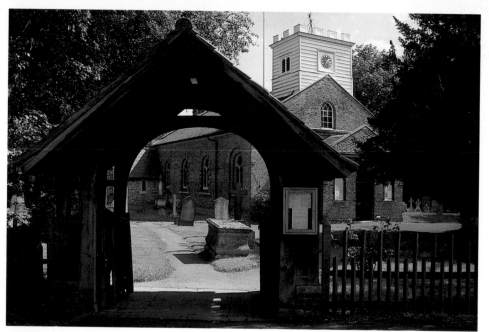

The parish church at Totteridge.

8 At Highwood Hill, opposite the Rising Sun pub, signed Mill Hill, turn left and ride steeply down then up Holcombe Hill – is this north London's only hairpin? – to the smart Ridgeway. After 1km, past the Hammers Pub, private schools, stables and churches, turn right carefully into Mill Hill High Street, just after the white buildings of Mill Hill boys public school and just before the road narrows between the houses.

9 This is old Mill Hill village with its pond, church and village sign. A 17th-century timbered Quaker meeting house sits on the main road behind the church. Turn right down 1km-long Milespit Hill and continue at the bottom to Pursley Road. Turn left, over the bridge, and, at the bottom of the slope, turn right carefully into Ashley Lane.

Take the bridleway track at the end, through Hendon golf course, and follow it up to the road and to the Great North Way dual carriageway at the end. Turn right on to the residential side road parallel with the main road as far as the footbridge.

10 Cross on the bridge (quite a view), and turn right on the other side downhill. At the subway after 400m, turn left into Sunny Hill Park. Turn right just inside the park and keep to the right-hand, western edge, all the way round for 1km, climbing at the end to leave the park on the track to the left of St Mary's churchyard, Church Terrace, leading to old Hendon village. Turn right past the shops for a look at the 17th-century Church Farm Museum of local history, the 19th-century Greyhound pub and St Mary's itself.

11 Turn back along Church End to the T-junction with Church Road, with almshouses opposite, and turn carefully right. The road becomes The Burroughs as it passes the Hendon site of Middlesex University, the ornate buildings of The Burroughs (Hendon Town Hall) and the library. After 500m turn left into Brampton Grove, and after 200m right into Wykeham Avenue. Continue to the bottom and turn left into Queens Road with Hendon Park on your right.

12 Continue along the top of the park to the far edge, then cross the road and take the track down the left-hand side of the park. Continue to the water fountain, then fork right across the centre of the park and head down to the fencing of the Northern Line in the right-hand, south-west corner. Leave the park at the bottom and turn right on Shirehall Lane to close the circle.

Mill Hill village pond, before the long descent of Milespit Hill.

Kew, Ham and Richmond

Four stately homes, herds of deer in Richmond Park, a foot ferry across the Thames and plenty of car-free riding make this west London mountain-bike tour a delight. The hills and traffic are not too bad, but the issue of cycling in Richmond Park and on the riverside is sensitive, so be considerate of walkers, only ride on the designated tracks, and do dismount where you are told to. In particular, on the riverbank north from Marble Hill House cyclists are under scrutiny from the Council to see whether we can share the space peacefully with walkers and whether cycling will be allowed there in the long term. Over to you.

Take some change to pay the ferryman (40p adults, 40p adult's bike, 20p child, 20p child's bike) who operates the foot ferry across the Thames between Ham and Marble Hill Houses.

Richmond Park offers car-free riding along the magnificent 11km shared cycle/walking circuit that runs around the outside edge of the entire Park – worth a trip in itself. Our route (marked in yellow and mauve) follows the track for 4km (Ride 14 uses it as well), but you may want to ride more of it to enjoy the Park's tranquil atmosphere.

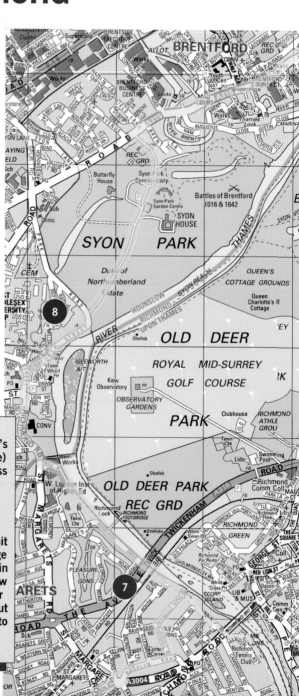

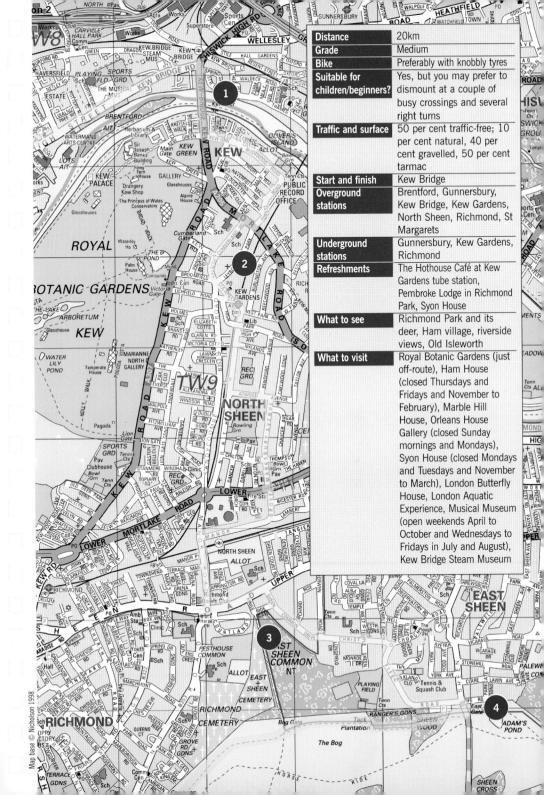

Distance	20km
Grade	Medium
Bike	Preferably with knobbly tyres
Suitable for children/beginners?	Yes, but you may prefer to dismount at a couple of busy crossings and several right turns
Traffic and surface	50 per cent traffic-free; 10 per cent natural, 40 per cent gravelled, 50 per cent tarmac
Start and finish	Kew Bridge
Overground stations	Brentford, Gunnersbury, Kew Bridge, Kew Gardens, North Sheen, Richmond, St Margarets
Underground stations	Gunnersbury, Kew Gardens, Richmond
Refreshments	The Hothouse Café at Kew Gardens tube station, Pembroke Lodge in Richmond Park, Syon House
What to see	Richmond Park and its deer, Ham village, riverside views, Old Isleworth
What to visit	Royal Botanic Gardens (just off-route), Ham House (closed Thursdays and Fridays and November to February), Marble Hill House, Orleans House Gallery (closed Sunday mornings and Mondays), Syon House (closed Mondays and Tuesdays and November to March), London Butterfly House, London Aquatic Experience, Musical Museum (open weekends April to October and Wednesdays to Fridays in July and August), Kew Bridge Steam Museum

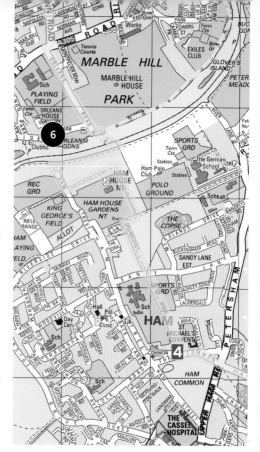

1 Starting at Kew Bridge, which has been targeted for upgrading for cyclists in the distant future, take the first left on the south bank alongside Kew Green, past the Greyhound pub. (For the Royal Botanic Gardens, take the first right after the bridge.) Continue straight on, with the pond on your right, taking the right fork ahead into Bushwood Road. (Although cyclists continually ride the riverbank path, officially this is illegal.)

At the end of Bushwood Road, go right into Forest Road and, at the end, cross busy Mortlake Road (zebra-crossing). Turn right and almost immediately go left into one-way Cumberland Road. (If you are riding the route anti-clockwise, you will come up Leyborne Park to emerge at this point.) At the end, turn left in to Kew Gardens Road and immediately left again in to Station Approach to the quaint parade of shops and cafés at Kew Gardens station.

2 Take the steps to the right of the station that lead over the railway bridge to North Road. Go right and continue for 500m, then turn left into Atwood Road. Take the first right into Marksbury Avenue, follow it to the end, and there cross busy Lower Richmond Road at the pelican crossing. Continue straight ahead into Manor Grove, bearing round to the right to Manor Road. Turn left, cross the level crossing, and continue to the lights on the busy A205 Sheen Road. Turn left at the lights and, with care, turn right after 400m (zebra crossing) into Sheen Common Drive.

3 Continue straight ahead for 500m, to Christ Church Road. After another 500m go right into Fife Road at the mini-roundabout. After 600m you will arrive at the grand gates of Richmond Park. Originally the Park was a royal hunting-ground, and still has large herds of deer. Go through the nearest pedestrian gate and see the yellowy gravelled shared walking/cycling track ahead of you.

4 Yippee, you are now off-road for a while. Follow the track to the right, anti-clockwise, around the park for 4km, crossing the road at Richmond Gate, passing Pembroke Lodge (with its fine tea terrace). Drop down the hill, and turn right at the bottom to exit at Ham Gate.

5 Leaving the Park, continue for 1km all the way along Ham Gate Avenue. A cycle route is promised some time in the future along the track on the right-hand verge. At the traffic-light junction with Upper Ham Road, cross straight over and after

200m leave the tarmac again and turn right at the white fencing along a bridleway. After 500m cross straight over Sandy Lane and continue in the same direction along the bridleway marked as Melancholy Walk, with Ham House in the distance.

At the brick wall that marks the perimeter of the grounds, dog-leg right and continue on the bridleway down the right-hand wall of the house for 300m. At the end turn left and pass in front of the handsome north front of the house to the road, Ham Street. The House, built in 1610 and enlarged in the 1670s, was once considered one of the finest in the land; there are restored 17th-century gardens and, inside, fine furniture and paintings. Back on the tarmac, turn right and head for the river through the car park. Once at the riverbank, turn right and watch out after 500m for Hammerton's foot ferry.

6 Hail the ferryman and he will come across and pick you up. The ferry runs on weekdays between February and October from 10am to 6pm

Map base © Nicholson 1998

and at weekends all year from 10am to 6.30pm or dusk. It may also not run during part of November while the sluices at Richmond are lifted. These maintain a stable water level – without them the river above Richmond would return to its tidal cycle, and at low tide the mighty Thames here would become a little trickle, leaving the ferry high and dry.

On the north bank of the river, to the left of the ferry mooring is Orleans House Gallery; of the original house only the octagon, built in 1720, still stands. At the mooring presides the ornate Marble Hill House, built for the mistress of George II in the mid-1720s.

Warren Footpath, the riverbank track from here north-eastwards for 1.5km to Richmond Bridge, is a scalding hot potato of access rights. Cycling has been temporarily allowed as a pilot scheme along a shared-use path, so walkers have priority and you must be prepared to dismount at busy times and be courteous. Only if there are no

Good cycling practice in Richmond Park

The Park is a unique area of grass and woodland and also a Site of Special Scientific Interest, where centuries of protection has produced habitats for rare flora and fauna. Mountain bikes cut up the grasslands, so please only ride on designated cycle paths and roads.

- Please be courteous to other Park users.
- Please give way to horses and walkers. Cyclists approaching quietly from behind can surprise other path users. Make sure they hear you coming well before you overtake – saying 'Hello' is simple and friendly.
- Ride carefully when you pass. Leave as much room as possible between yourself and walkers and horses. Do not try to squeeze past.
- Bunching is harassing. Please ride no more than two abreast.
- Dogs must be kept under control at all times. The Royal Parks discourage dogs running with cycles.
- Be tidy. Please take your litter home and guard against fire.

Leave Richmond Park through Ham Gate.

complaints will cycling be permitted here permanently.

At Richmond Bridge, go up the slipway, cross over Richmond Road at the pelican lights and go head into Willoughby Road. (Richmond town centre, with its shops and cafés, lies on the far side of the river.) Observe the No Cycling and Dismount signs through the alleyways as far as Ducks Walk, and follow this to Twickenham Bridge.

For the officially preferred, cycle-signed street route, continue for 500m up Orleans Road to the end, turn right carefully across Richmond Road and go left into Crown Road. Just before you hit the main road at the end, turn right – take care once again – into short King's Road, to St Margarets Road. Turn right here, and take the second left into Rosslyn Road. Take the third left, Riverdale Road, then turn right at the end into Riverdale Gardens and head down to Ducks Walk on the river. Turn left and, observing the No Cycling and Dismount signs, emerge at Twickenham Bridge.

7 Go beneath Twickenham Bridge into Ranelagh Drive, past Richmond Lock (the limit of the tidal Thames), and at the end follow the signed cycle path hard along the river. Leave the river at Railshead Road and turn right at the end on to the busy Richmond Road. Continue for 500m, then, on the left-hand bend in Isleworth, turn right carefully into Upper Square and North Street. Take the first right into Manor House Way, and then turn left at the end into Church Street along the quaint riverfront of Old Isleworth. After 500m turn right into Syon Park.

8 Follow the road for 1km to Syon House. Here there are numerous attractions, including the house itself and its gardens, with a handsome glass-domed conservatory, the London Butterfly House, the London Aquatic Experience, shops, a café and a fine health-food store for in-the-saddle-snacks. On reaching the car park, stay straight ahead, and head out the far side of the estate between the narrowing brick walls.

At the main London Road turn carefully right and continue for 2km over the end of the River Brent navigation at Brentford Locks, through Brentford town and past Waterman's Arts Centre on the right. On the left are the Musical Museum, which specialises in mechanical reproducers of music, and then Kew Bridge Steam Museum, where steam engines used for water supply are displayed. At Kew Bridge you must shift into the right-hand lane to turn right to cross the river.

Part of the lovely 'yellow brick road' around the park.

Wimbledon Common and Richmond Park

This is a quick, largely car-free trip around three of urban London's lovely wild places: Wimbledon Common, Putney Heath and Richmond Park. The highlights are Wimbledon's windmill and Richmond's deer, plus a spin through the modernist Roehampton estate, which has been listed as an important example of 1950s architecture.

The paths you can ride are clearly defined, so please keep to these tracks and observe good cycling practice.

Distance	10km
Grade	Easy – off-road
Bike	Mountain bike
Suitable for children/beginners?	Yes, lots of natural land, with mostly quiet roads
Traffic and surface	90 per cent traffic-free, 40 per cent natural
Start and finish	Tibbet's Corner
Overground stations	Barnes, Putney, Richmond, Wimbledon
Underground stations	East Putney, Richmond, Southfields, Wimbledon
Refreshments	Wimbledon Common, Richmond Park, the Telegraph pub near Tibbet's Corner
What to see	Wimbledon Common, Richmond Park, Roehampton estate
What to visit	Wimbledon Windmill Museum (open afternoons on summer weekends and public holidays)

1 At Tibbet's Corner roundabout, at the junction of the A3 and Wimbledon Park Side, enter the subway, following the subway cycle signs for Wimbledon and Southfields. Exit at the sign for Wimbledon Common up a wide, tarmac track that leads directly on to the Common. Continue on the Common straight ahead for 1km to the windmill and café. The Windmill Museum is devoted to the history of windmills, and has many working models.

2 With the windmill to your right, continue on the wide gravel track straight ahead for another 1km.

This route uses another section of Richmond Park's 12km shared path.

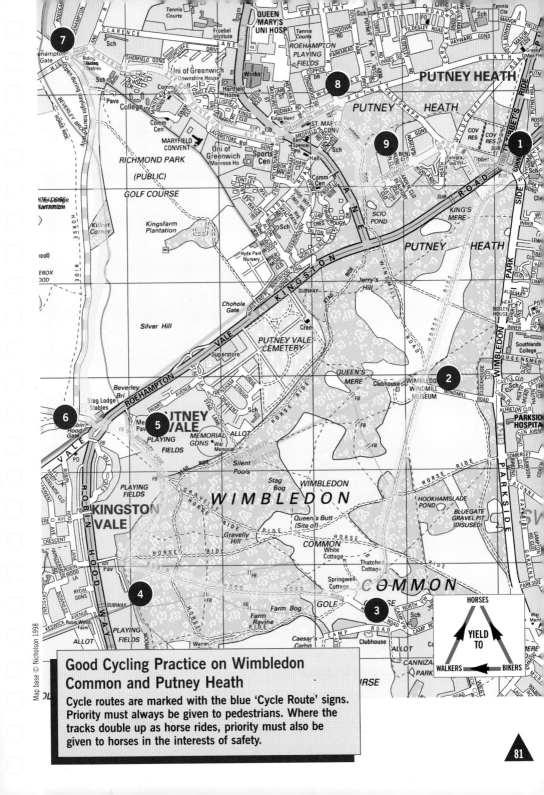

Good Cycling Practice on Wimbledon Common and Putney Heath

Cycle routes are marked with the blue 'Cycle Route' signs. Priority must always be given to pedestrians. Where the tracks double up as horse rides, priority must also be given to horses in the interests of safety.

Map base © Nicholson 1998

3 Bear right at a grassy triangle with white stones and take the white gate to the left of the white cottage. Continue for 1km to the bottom of the track.

4 Turn right at the brick bridge and ride along the river, known as Beverley Brook.

5 At the brick changing-rooms at the end, turn left over another brick bridge and exit the common at Robin Hood roundabout. Cross over by the footbridge and enter Richmond Park beside the stables. (Ignore the 'no cycles' sign on the bridge. There are no breaks in the traffic and this is the only way to cross the road!)

6 Inside the Park, turn immediately right anticlockwise on to the shared cycling/walking path (marked in yellow and mauve) that runs 11km around the perimeter of the park. Continue for 2km to Roehampton Gate. (There is a cafe behind the car park.)

7 Leave the park at the Roehampton Gate. Take the first right into Danebury Lane and climb 1km up through Roehampton estate to the main road, Roehampton Lane. Following cycle signs for Southfields and Wimbledon, cross straight ahead at the lights up little Roehampton High Street.

8 Emerge at the top on to Putney Heath. Take the second right (one way), and after 50m on the right-hand bend turn on to the Common along a clearly marked cycle track. Continue for 500m.

9 Fork right at the grass arena, turn left at Scio Pond and return to tarmac on Portsmouth Road. At the T-junction at the end, turn right into Telegraph Road. Then continue straight across past the Telegraph pub on the cycle path, and follow the path around to the left to the subway under Tibbet's Corner.

Good Cycling Practice in Richmond Park

The Park is a unique area of grass and woodland and also a Site of Special Scientific Interest, where centuries of protection has produced habitats for rare flora and fauna. Mountain bikes cut up the grasslands, so please only ride on designated cycle paths and roads.

- Please be courteous to other Park users.
- Please give way to horses and walkers. Cyclists approaching quietly from behind can surprise other path users. Make sure they hear you coming well before you overtake – saying 'Hello' is simple and friendly.
- Ride carefully when you pass. Leave as much room as possible between yourself and walkers and horses. Do not try to squeeze past.
- Bunching is harassing. Please ride no more than two abreast.
- Dogs must be kept under control at all times. The Royal Parks discourage dogs running with cycles.
- Be tidy. Please take your litter home and guard against fire.

Feeling tired? Lean on a horse! Two 'mounties' on Wimbledon Common, with the windmill and museum in the background. Teas are served just around the corner.

Three Commons and the Wandle

Yesterday's neglected brookside is tomorrow's nature reserve, as proved by the fabulous Wandle Trail along the River Wandle on the western half of this green-based mountain-bike circuit. For 4km from Colliers Wood to Wandsworth town just one short section is a footpath where you should walk. Eventually the Trail will run all the way to Sutton so you can explore the tributary much further south.

The eastern half of this ride links three much-loved London commons: Clapham, Wandsworth and Tooting, each used to capacity in the summer. At publication the route uses tracks on Tooting and Wandsworth commons which are not legally ridable. However, these are supposed to be upgraded to cycle paths during 1998. Until then please walk your bike along these tracks, they are shown on the map in a dashed line.

Distance	14km
Grade	Easy
Bike	Preferably with knobbly tyres
Suitable for children/beginners?	Yes, with care on the roads, most of which either have cycle paths or are backstreets. There is lots of good traffic-free tracks and parkland
Traffic and surface	50 per cent traffic-free, all surfaced
Start and finish	Clapham Common
Overground stations	Balham, Clapham Junction, Earlsfield, Haydons Road, Streatham, Tooting, Wandsworth Common, Wandsworth Town, Wimbledon
Underground stations	Wimbledon, Wimbledon Park
Refreshments	Cafés on Clapham and Tooting commons
What to see	Wandsworth Prison, Wimbledon FC stadium, Amen Corner, Wandle Meadows nature reserve

1 Enter Clapham Common on foot on its western side, half-way along The Avenue, and walk along the track to the bandstand. There, turn right on to the cycle route that runs north–south on the far side. At Windmill Drive turn briefly left, signposted for Tooting, then at the signpost turn right back on to the cycle track as far as Clapham Common South Side.

2 Cross over and go straight ahead along Narbonne Road, taking the second right into Abbeville Road. At the end turn left briefly into Poynders Road. Then, dismounting if you prefer, take care as you cross to the right-hand lane, and go straight ahead at the lights into Cavendish Road. Continue for 1km to the mini-roundabout at the start of Tooting Common before the railway arch.

3 Go under the arch and pick up the track through the Common. Plans are afoot to upgrade these tracks to shared cycle/walking paths, but until that happens you should walk the bike to

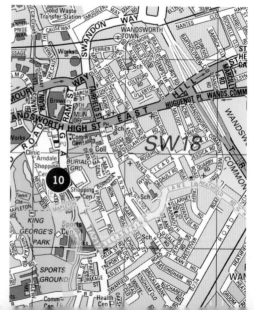

the far side of the Common. Continue under the second arch and alongside the houses to Bedford Hill. Cross over. Go immediately straight ahead, then left at the fork near the café to Tooting Bec Road.

4 Cross Tooting Bec Road and take the track to the right of Tooting athletics track, where you should continue to walk. Where it meets the road (Church Lane), bear to the left and stay on the track as far as Furzedown Road. Turn right to the roundabout and there take the well-marked cycle route down Rectory Lane for 1km.

5 At the lights at the end, at Amen Corner, dog-leg right (into Southcroft Road) and left at the main lights into Mitcham Road. Continue for 500m to Tooting station. Take the first right beyond the station, Finborough Road. At the end, waggle your way around Flanders Crescent, turn right into Swains Road and go under the house through the metal barrier to emerge at Robinson Road.

6 Continue along Robinson Road for 500m, then turn left at the main Colliers Wood road. Take the sixth right, Byegrove Road, and continue for 250m to the corner with Denison Road.

7 There take the track signposted as a footpath for Summerstown. It is here that this routes joins the Wandle Trail, which follows the Wandle river northwards to the Thames. After walking the bike along the short section of footpath from Byegrove Road to North Road, you are free to ride for the next 4km to Wandsworth.

The route follows the River Wandle for 4km.

(At Boundary Road ignore the cycle sign for Summerstown and Plough Lane and continue straight ahead.) Cross over North Road and continue on the track alongside the houses. Take the signposted track (Mead Path) at the end and continue undisturbed for 1km to Plough Lane.

Map base © Nicholson 1998

8 Turn left on the road just to cross the bridge and, on the far side, pick up the track again, now on the left bank of the river. Continue (Wimbledon FC is on the left) for a little over 1km to the end. Cross the river, take the first road on the left, Summerley Street, and follow that to Garratt Lane.

Turn left, pass beneath the railway bridge and take the second left at the traffic lights into Penwith Road. Take the first left into Ravensbury Terrace and first right into Ravensbury Road. Take the first right into Acuba Road. (This avoids most of Penwith Road, which is a busy cut-through for cars, and cuts out the right turn on to Acuba Road.) At the end enter King George's Park.

9 Inside the park, stay on the paths near the river for a little over 1km, riding considerately of people, children and dogs. Cross over at the cycle lights at Kimber Road and continue as far as Wandle Recreation Centre. Here, turn right out of the park into Mapleton Road.

10 Turn right on to Garratt Lane, watching the traffic, and take the first true left into Allfarthing Lane. Follow this pretty road for about 1km as it becomes Heathfield Road, crosses Earlsfield Road and runs alongside the back of Wandsworth nick. Just beyond the prison turn left into Alma Terrace and cross busy Trinity Road.

11 Continue straight ahead into Dorlcote Road. At the corner at the end, walk the bike on to the track on to Wandsworth Common, first alongside the housing, then bearing diagonally right to the bridge over the railway line. You should walk the bike as these tracks are in the lengthy process of being turned into shared cycle/walking paths. Over the bridge, continue on the straight-ahead track to the road at Bolingbroke Grove, and turn right.

12 Stay on the footpath along the Common as far as the crossing opposite Thurleigh Road, and cross (this will be a cycle toucan crossing). Ride 1km all the way along Thurleigh Road to the end and turn left into Clapham Common West Side.

After 300m, turn right into Broomwood Road, cross over the Avenue and go ahead, walking the bike again, on to Clapham Common.

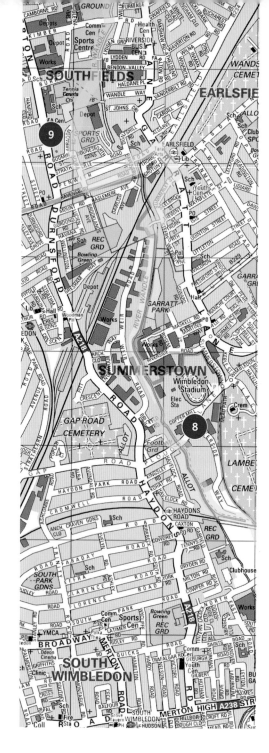

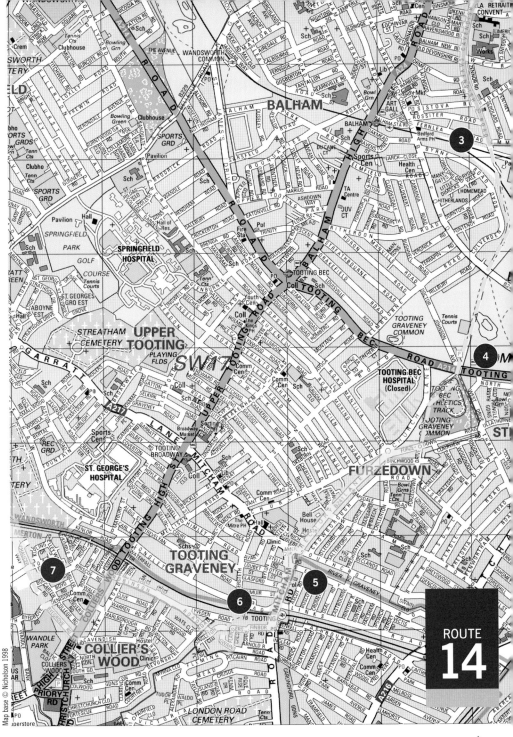

ROUTE
14

ROUTE 15

THE SUBURBS

Herne Hill to Greenwich
via the Ravensbourne

Interesting features come thick and fast on this varied route for road bikes, which mostly runs along cycle paths and through parkland. Starting at Herne Hill Velodrome (built in 1892 and the site of the cycling events in the 1948 Olympic Games) and finishing at Greenwich, it climbs for nearly 90m through genteel Dulwich to the top of the hill at Crystal Palace, then loses height passing through the National Sports Centre before jumping across to Beckenham Place Park using a Bromley Borough cycle route. From here the ride turns distinctly greener as it joins Ravensbourne River, one of the pretty little Thames tributaries. For 7km you follow this babbling brook northwards through nature reserves, playing fields and handsome backstreets to its mouth at Deptford Creek on the Thames. We tried to find a good way of completing the loop back from Greenwich to Herne Hill, but couldn't. Any suggestions appreciated....

Distance	17km
Grade	Medium – 90m climb up to Crystal Palace
Bike	Preferably with smooth tyres
Suitable for children/beginners?	Yes. There is a lot of traffic-free riding with few major roads, though the hill is big
Traffic and surface	30 per cent traffic-free, all surfaced
Start and finish	Herne Hill Velodrome to Greenwich riverfront
Overground stations	Herne Hill (start), Greenwich (finish)
Refreshments	Dulwich Village, Crystal Palace Park, Greenwich
What to see	Herne Hill Velodrome, National Sports Centre and Crystal Palace Park, Riverview Park, Ravensbourne river, Greenwich
What to visit	Dulwich Picture Gallery
Notes	For maps of cycle routes in the Borough of Bromley, including the Crystal Palace–Bromley route used here, contact the Transportation Support Team, Technical Services, Bromley Civic Centre, Stockwell Close, Bromley BR1 3UH

1 From Herne Hill stadium, turn left eastwards on to Burbage Road and continue for 500m to the memorial roundabout at Dulwich Village.

2 Turn right into College Road and, passing Dulwich Picture Gallery, England's oldest picture gallery with a fine collection of Old Masters, climb gradually straight ahead for 2.5km, through the toll gate (free for bikes) up to the top of the hill. At the top, turn right carefully on to Crystal Palace Parade. At the roundabout after 1km, turn left down Anerley Hill.

3 After 250m of steep downhill, sweep left into the entrance to the National Sports Centre. Follow the LCN signs down the hill and around the southern end of the athletics track. Beyond the stadium, follow the LCN sign pointing right across Crystal Palace Park. At the red finger-post sign turn left and follow the cycle track to the edge of the park (Sydenham Hill Gate, locked at night, closing times vary summer and winter) on Crystal Palace Park Road, then turn right down the hill.

4 Stay on the main road as it becomes Penge High Street beyond the railway arches. Then take the fourth left into St John's Road. This brings you to the start of a 2.5km-stretch of sign-posted Bromley Borough cycle route. Very soon, take the second right into Queen Adelaide Road, and soon again thereafter turn left on to Penge Lane. Turn right at the end on to Parish Lane. After 250m turn left into Tennyson Road, take the first right-hand turn soon into Somerville Road and almost immediately the first left into Courtenay Road.

At the end turn right into Lennard Road and continue for 800m to New Beckenham Station.

88

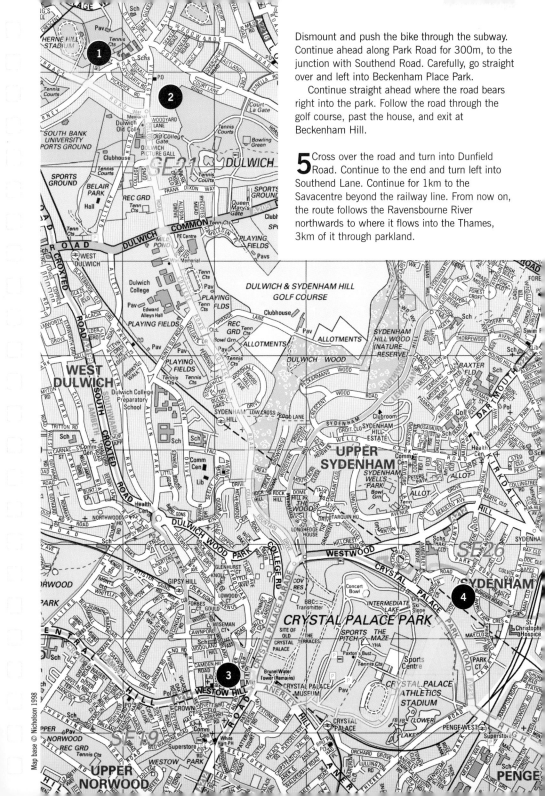

Dismount and push the bike through the subway. Continue ahead along Park Road for 300m, to the junction with Southend Road. Carefully, go straight over and left into Beckenham Place Park.

Continue straight ahead where the road bears right into the park. Follow the road through the golf course, past the house, and exit at Beckenham Hill.

5 Cross over the road and turn into Dunfield Road. Continue to the end and turn left into Southend Lane. Continue for 1km to the Savacentre beyond the railway line. From now on, the route follows the Ravensbourne River northwards to where it flows into the Thames, 3km of it through parkland.

6 On the right, turn into Riverview Walk beside the Ravensbourne, a stunning piece of aqua-landscaping that includes areas for plants to thrive and banks and bridges for people to enjoy. Continue to the end, then stay with the humbler riverbank for another 1km to exit at Catford Road.

7 Walking on the pavement, turn right, pass beneath the railway bridge, and then take unsigned Adenmore Road. This turns off at the entrance to Ravensbourne Park to run 50m parallel to the main road, between the two stations. (Eventually, the river path will continue uninterrupted beneath the bridges.) Turn left at the end under the railway arch, then first right into Bourneville Road and into Ladywell Fields.

8 Stay alongside the river for 1km, past Catford dog track, over the railway line via the green spiral bridge, and past the old athletics track.

9 Emerge on Ladywell Road. Turn left over the bridge, take the first right, Algernon Road, then the first right, Marsala Road, and right again under the railway bridge into Elmira Street. Emerge at busy Loampit Vale.

10 Cross the road, and go straight ahead into Thurston Road on the cycle path. Follow that on to Brookmill Road, which runs alongside Brookmill Park, which was closed at publication. (The park should reopen in about 1999, once the Docklands Light Railway extension has been built. A walk- and cycle-way will be installed through the park).

11 At the busy A2, Deptford Broadway, go straight ahead into Deptford Church Street and take the first right, Creekside, where light industry hides the route from the now tidal river. After 500m turn right again into Copperas Street. Turn right at the end into Creek Road, and you will see that the babbling Ravensbourne has turned into a large tidal flow that fills Deptford Creek. Take the first left into Norway Street and follow the Thames Path signs to the riverfront at Greenwich.

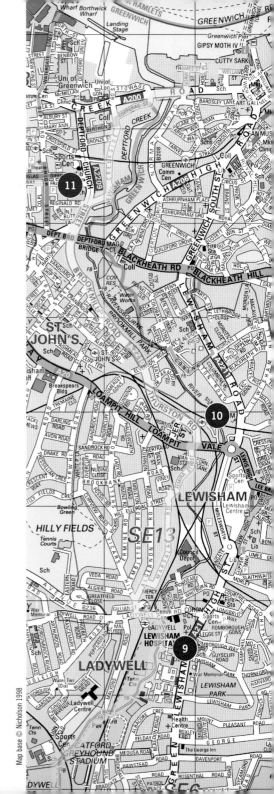

Map base © Nicholson 1998

Country
rides

Into Essex

Who would have believed that such a rural idyll exists the London side of the M25? By using the ridable tracks in three country parks – Hainault, Havering and Bedfords – and bridleways through Curtismill Green, this long circuit provides a taste of true countryside and a memorable mountain bike work-out. A pleasant alternative for children is simply to explore the country parks.

Starting from Hainault Forest Country Park – where there is some super riding – we cross off-road to Havering Country Park, then hop via picturesque Havering village to Bedfords Park and use backroads to get to Curtismill Green's woodland tracks. The final piece of sweet off-road begins at the tranquil hamlet of Lambourne, with its white clapboard church and hall. Ride it, and Essex will never feel quite the same again.

Distance	26km
Grade	Medium to difficult – hilly and potentially very muddy
Bike	Mountain bike
Suitable for children/beginners?	Possibly. There is a lot of rural off-road riding, but much of it is hard going. Perhaps it is better to stick to ridable routes in Hainault Forest and Havering Country Parks
Traffic and surface	50 per cent off-road, much natural surface, some roads, no major crossings
Start and finish	Hainault Forest car park on Manor Road, Chigwell Row
Overground stations	Harold Wood, Romford
Underground stations	Hainault (Central Line – access only from Leyton and stations eastwards at off-peak times)
Refreshments	The Camelot pub (Manor Road), Teas on the Green (Havering village), The Tea Shop, Crowther Nurseries, Lambourne
What to see	Idyllic rural scene, including village greens, churches, brooks, stables, pheasants, rabbits, squirrels and birdlife, stocks on Havering village green, and planes at Stapleford airfield

Previous page: The off-road link between Hainault Forest and Havering Country Parks.

Left: Havering-atte-Bower village.

1 Start at the car park on Manor Road, on the northern edge of Hainault Forest Country Park, and take the main shared horse/bike track along the fence towards the forest. Continue in the same direction for 400m to a track T-junction and turn right, on the horsetrack parallel to the walking track marked with the green arrows. Continue in the same direction for 600m, changing tracks near the end to get to the dual carriageway. Here turn left. Continue for 1km, ignoring the main entrance to the park, and carrying on up the hill. At the bus stop at the top, take the track back into the park through the gap in the fence to the left.

2 Head uphill, picking up the track along the edge of the park. Stay high along the fencing for 1km, and then drop down to the park buildings. Continue straight over the road, picking up the grass horse/bike track on the left marked with the green arrow. Now get ready to climb hard. Continue to a T-junction, then turn right. Soon, at the signboard, dog-leg left to continue in the same direction for 1km down a rough slope – control your speed – emerging over a bridge at an open field, at the end of the Country Park.

Both Hainault and Havering Country Parks have a network of ridable horsetracks which bikes may share. Signboards in Hainault and signs en route in Havering show where they are, as do leaflets available from both park offices. Mind walkers and horses, and limit your speed on the slopes, some of which are long. Please be considerate on all the bridleways at all times, especially as local horseriders have expressed concern about the increased number of cyclists. Ride considerately and they will have no complaint. Hainault Park has worked with local mountain bikers to put together this code of conduct:

• Ride only on permissive cycleways
• Give way to horses
• Be considerate of other users
• Take your litter home
• Do not use waterlogged rides

A note on mud. In winter and after rain, with so much natural track this circuit could be the gloopiest in the collection. Please observe Hainault Park's request not to ride on waterlogged tracks. Good luck!

© Crown Copyright

Note: After wet weather this ride is potentially impassable in dozens of places!

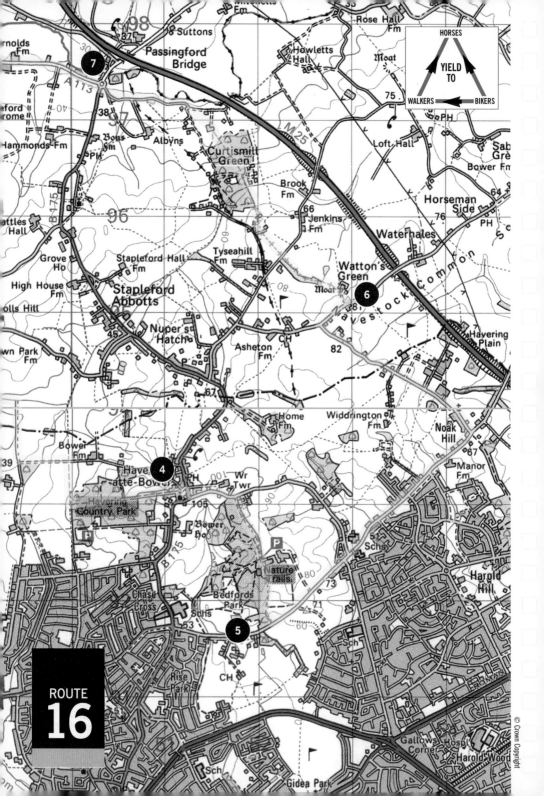

Billy of Crowther Nurseries.

3 Now comes the link to Havering Park. Continue in the same direction for 500m, then turn right on the farm road, and continue along here for 500m. Turn left at a sign saying 'Horseriders please keep to bridleway path' (this means bikers too). Ride as far as another junction below the farmhouse and turn right. After 500m turn up the second left (not the first track with the 'Havering Country Park' sign) and enter the woods of the park on the shared horse/bike track. Prepare for another rough climb. Ride for 500m to the five-ways junction, then continue in the same direction, signed 'Village' to leave the Park at Havering village, past the stables, to the green with its summertime teashop and church.

4 Turn right on to the road along the green, and at the junction at the end (near the stocks), turn left along Broxhill Road, for Harold Hill, towards the handsome water tower. After 500m, just before the tower, turn right carefully into Bedfords Park. Continue in the same direction, dropping down through the park on tarmac and a deteriorating track that narrows at the bottom, to emerge at a busy road, signed 'Bridleway and Byway No 23'. See description on page 98 for a possible alternative route between Havering and Bedfords Park.

5 Turn left on to what is the busiest road on the circuit, so take care for the next 2.5km as you continue on the same road until you pass clapboard and thatched houses and reach a left turn (at Noak Hill), signed 'Church Road for St Thomas's Church'. Take this turning, and continue for 2km to the T-junction at Navestock Common. Turn right, continue for 300m, then turn left at the sign for Dycotts Farm and get ready for some single track.

6 Follow the gravel road to the farmgate, then stay as it turns left. At the entrance to the golf course, take the lightly-marked grass track (a RUPP, a road used as a public path) off to the left. Follow this rough track straight over at a gravel cross-track for the golf course, and stay with it down towards the thicket. Here, where the tracks diverge, take the left-hander for an easier ride.

Continue on this single track all the way to a little road, cross over and continue (now on a BOAT,

Epping Forest District Council Planning Department has informed us that a new off-road link between Havering and Bedfords Park has recently been negotiated with a local landowner. It is not marked on this map, nor did we ride it, but the directions go something like this: In Havering Park at the five-ways junction go right (not straight on as marked on the map), continue to a T-junction trail, turn left into Pinewood Road, and continue to the B175 road out of Havering-atte-Bower. Find the track somewhere on the other side of the road that enters Bower Park and skirts Bower House to meet up with the route again on the track through Bedfords Park.

a byway open to all traffic) all the way to another little road. Pick that up briefly, then take the track again off to the left near the cottages. Continue into the woods, now on a bridleway. The tracks through Curtismill Green woods are clear, but which of them is the mapped bridleway is not, so continue in the same direction following your nose as best you can. At another little road, turn left and pick up a track on the right after 100m.

After 500m of rough riding, emerge on the commonland of Curtismill Green, close to the M25. Follow tracks round to the left, the north-west, and pick up one of the roads that serves the scattered houses. Head along the road in the same direction and after 1km emerge at a roundabout.

7 Go straight over on to the A113, for Abridge, and continue for 2.5km past Stapleford airfield and the Tea Shop, Crowther Nurseries (cream teas). Beyond them, take the left turn for Lambourne Church. After 1.5km climbing you reach beautiful Lambourne hamlet. The church dates back to the 12th century – you can see the blocked-off Norman doors on the north and south walls of the nave. Lambourne Hall dates from the 16th century.

Return to the first house, and find the bridleway through the field to its left (not across its lawn) and along the hedge.

8 Continue up here for 1km, emerge on the road, turn right into Manor Road, and continue for 1km to the Camelot pub at Lambourne End. Take the left-hand turn opposite the pub back into Hainault Forest Country Park.

9 Continue for 500m in the same direction on the shared horse/bike path, as far as the open sward with the signboard on the left. Turn right on the rough horsetrack and ride for 1km as far as a right-turn with a green arrow. Retrace your pedalstrokes back to the car park on Manor Road.

There's good off-road riding in the country parks on the Essex border. This is Hainault Forest. Watch for people and horses – and puddles.

Epping Forest

Leap astride your mountain bike to flee the modern world for ancient woodland where Henry VIII and Queen Elizabeth once hunted for deer. Mystical Epping Forest forms the largest acreage of mountain-bikable land within the area covered by this book. Apart from a few protected features (including the embankments of Ambresbury Banks to the north, Loughton Camp and the meanders of Loughton Brook to the east), you can ride freely anywhere you like – you don't even have to keep to the tracks. So get to know the forest's charm on this circuit, then strike forth to discover its secret pockets and fine riding for yourself.

This ride boasts a handful of steep roller-coasters that will test less fit riders and give experienced ones a work-out. But watch your speed. A couple of the busiest sections are on descents, and walkers and horse-riders love the forest too, so it can be a busy place on a sunny Sunday. It can be more enjoyable to visit midweek or on a Saturday.

Distance	17km
Grade	Medium – steep undulations and loose surfaces
Bike	Mountain bike
Suitable for children/beginners?	Yes, all off-road but hard work
Traffic and surface	Totally traffic-free; 50 per cent natural, 50 per cent gravel surface, potentially gloriously muddy
Start and finish	Epping Forest Conservation Centre, High Beach
Overground stations	Chingford
Underground stations	Buckhurst Hill, Epping, Loughton, Theydon Bois. All these are on the Central Line; access only from Leyton and stations eastwards at off-peak times
Refreshments	King's Oak pub, High Beach; tea at Butler's Retreat adjoining Queen Elizabeth's Hunting Lodge; tea hut at Hill Wood
What to see	Ancient woodland, view into Hertfordshire from High Beach, ancient fort and embankments (no riding), the meanders of Loughton Brook (no riding), deer, rabbits and a cricket pitch over a motorway
What to visit	Queen Elizabeth's Hunting Lodge (open Wednesday to Sunday afternoons)

1 Start at Pillow Mounds car park at the Epping Forest Conservation Centre behind the King's Oak pub at High Beach. The Centre sells maps of the Forest and provides an introduction to its history and ecology.

Turn right on to the road from the Centre, and almost immediately left off the road through posts on to a surfaced ride, the General's Ride.

2 Cross Woodridden Hill and take the track to the right parallel with the road. Ignore the left-hand ride and continue round the back of the riding school. Continue over the little road to the busy B1393. Continue straight over that to the big junction of rides.

3 Turn left on to the Green Ride (going north), and continue for 500 undulating metres. The embankments of the ancient fort of Ambresbury Banks lie in the bushes on the left; take a look, but resist the temptation to ride, which is forbidden.

The next junction marks the start of a 2.5km loop which you can cut out if you wish. Following the loop anticlockwise, as shown on the map, continue for another 500m, and exit through a parking area to a road. The brick parapet opposite marks the entrance of the M25 motorway into a cut-and-cover tunnel that runs beneath the cricket pitch!

4 Turn back, taking the ride to the right, with the cricket ground on the right. Continue through the woods, then turn left back towards the main track this side of Ambresbury Banks to complete the loop. Rejoin the main track and continue.

5 Cross straight over the road, continue straight through the car park and then on to Ditches Ride. After 500m turn right on to Green Ride/Centenary Walk and continue. After another 500m, continue straight over another road and get ready for some dramatic roller-coastering – don't spook the people or horses with your speed – for another 2km.

6 Continue across the road, through the car park and past Strawberry Hill ponds. After 200m dog-leg on to the Three Forests Way to continue in the same direction to the white cottages of the Epping Forest Conservators.

7 Go past the black gate and take the right-hand track on to Warren Hill. Turn left at the little clearing at the top of the hill; it can be very muddy here. Continue as the track narrows and curves right and uphill to Manor Road.

8 Continue straight ahead through Powell's Forest, over the busy A104, and down a super grassy slope. At the bottom, continue, keeping Ranger's Road (A1069) on the right. Continue on by Butler's Retreat teahouse (refreshments available) and cross the road, turning back northwards. To the left of the teahouse stands the timber-framed Queen Elizabeth's Hunting Lodge, built by Henry VIII; there are displays on the history of Epping Forest and of the building.

9 Facing north-eastwards, take the posted ride slightly to the right and head downhill. Continue for 1km to a 'roundabout' junction. Fork left and then go straight ahead. Ignore the criss-crossing white-posted rides and follow the surfaced track for 1km, exiting at Hill Wood near the tea hut.

10 Continue over the road (Cross Roads) on to the Up and Down Ride for 1km, which is another dramatic roller-coaster – watch your speed. At the top of the final hill on the left is an 'easy access' path which we are asked not to ride – it is for people less able than ourselves. We stay on the hard ride back round to Pillow Mounds car park.

Explore Epping Forest freely by bike.

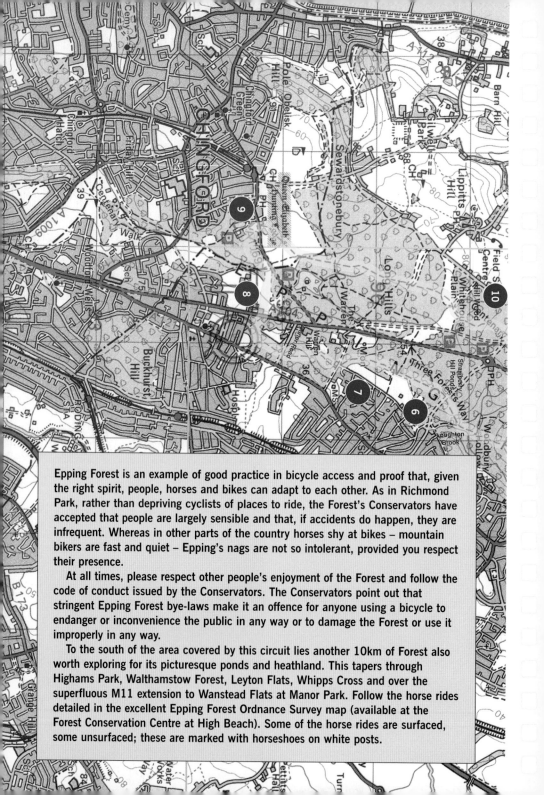

Epping Forest is an example of good practice in bicycle access and proof that, given the right spirit, people, horses and bikes can adapt to each other. As in Richmond Park, rather than depriving cyclists of places to ride, the Forest's Conservators have accepted that people are largely sensible and that, if accidents do happen, they are infrequent. Whereas in other parts of the country horses shy at bikes – mountain bikers are fast and quiet – Epping's nags are not so intolerant, provided you respect their presence.

At all times, please respect other people's enjoyment of the Forest and follow the code of conduct issued by the Conservators. The Conservators point out that stringent Epping Forest bye-laws make it an offence for anyone using a bicycle to endanger or inconvenience the public in any way or to damage the Forest or use it improperly in any way.

To the south of the area covered by this circuit lies another 10km of Forest also worth exploring for its picturesque ponds and heathland. This tapers through Highams Park, Walthamstow Forest, Leyton Flats, Whipps Cross and over the superfluous M11 extension to Wanstead Flats at Manor Park. Follow the horse rides detailed in the excellent Epping Forest Ordnance Survey map (available at the Forest Conservation Centre at High Beach). Some of the horse rides are surfaced, some unsurfaced; these are marked with horseshoes on white posts.

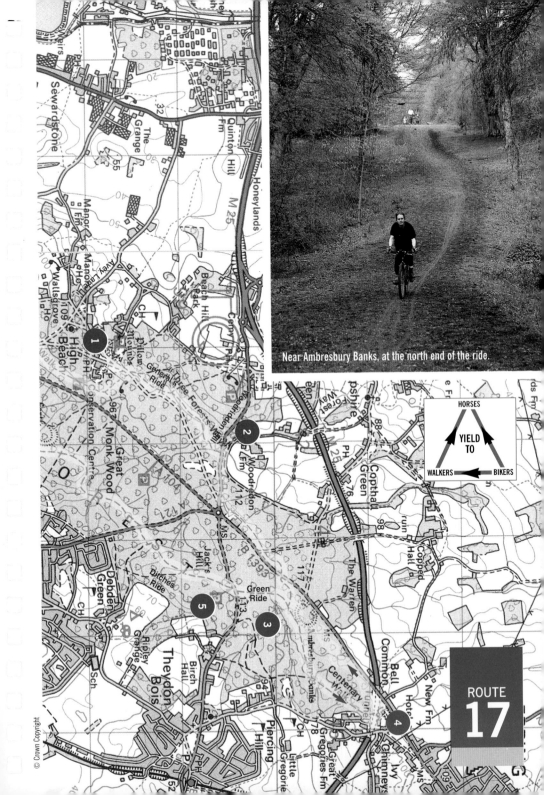

Near Ambresbury Banks, at the north end of the ride.

HORSES

YIELD
TO

WALKERS   BIKERS

ROUTE
17

Hadley Common and Trent Park

This pretty ride on London's northern border with Hertfordshire may be short, but it requires fitness and determination. On the ancient commonland of Monken Hadley, originally part of Enfield Chase where nobility hunted deer, the route passes four of the five listed white gates that marked the boundary of the Common and also the southern tip of a pond system filled by Monken Mead Brook. Leafy Trent Park, which is one of the sites of Middlesex University, has a bike trail that is surprisingly tough. It's the only real riding in the park, as pain-in-the-butt bikers have got cycling banned from everywhere else but on the roads. The park café serves good, basic food, which is some compensation.

Care is needed on the 2km section along busy Cockfosters Road.

Distance	12km
Grade	Medium – surprisingly hilly
Bike	Mountain bike
Suitable for children/beginners?	Yes, with reservations. The full ride is tough going and Cockfosters Road features fast lines of traffic
Traffic and surface	50 per cent off-road
Start and finish	Hadley Road, Hadley Wood
Overground stations	Hadley Wood, New Barnet
Refreshments	Cock and Dragon pub in Cockfosters and Trent Park café
What to see	Commonland, gates of old common boundary
Notes	Cycling is not allowed on Hadley Common or in Trent Park, except on roads and on the bike trail

1 Start at the junction of Hadley Road with Hadley Common/Bakers Hill, at the first set of white gates. Follow Bakers Hill eastwards and straight ahead for 2.5km as the road changes surface and status from tarmac to gravel to bridleway, passing over the main railway line (keep right) and the southern tip of Monken Hadley Ponds.

2 Leave Monken Hadley Common past a second set of white gates via Games Road, with the Cock and Dragon pub on your right, and exit at Chalk Lane on to the busy Cockfosters Road.

A misty, moisty morning beside Monken Hadley Common.

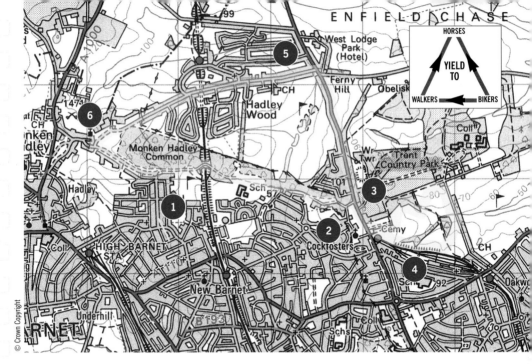

© Crown Copyright

3 Opposite is Trent Country Park. Cycling is allowed only on the official bike trail on the park's southern edge and on the roadways in the park, not on the footpaths or horsetrails.

4 The tough 4km mountain bike trail, marked with white-tipped posts and all on uncut grass, is open and hilly with a separate entrance from the main park. Two circuits are enough to wipe anyone out! Find it beside Cockfosters underground station 300m to the south along Cockfosters Road, where it runs along the north side of the station car park.
  Exit beside the tube station and turn right carefully on to the horribly busy Cockfosters Road. Continue, watching the traffic, for 1km.

5 At a staggered crossroads, turn left up Beech Hill and continue for 2km up through Hadley Wood village along a wide, pleasant road, becoming Camlet Way, past the third set of white gates.

6 At the T-junction with Hadley Common and white gate number four, turn left on to Hadley Common and complete the circuit to the junction with Hadley Road.

ROUTE 19

Pinner, Harrow Weald and Northwood

Sleepy, tree-lined residential streets and short pieces of bridleway mark this mountain-bike route around well-to-do Pinner and Northwood. Treading a path from pretty Pinner High Street via Pinner Park Farm on to the climb up to Harrow Weald and back to Ruislip Woods, it has a rural feel, boosted by some good off-road riding.

The climbs are tough for anyone unfit, and there are steep steps over the railway line north of Hatch End. However, the stretches on busy roads have been kept to a minimum. Unfortunately the climb up to the Weald has to be made on roads, as the pleasant bridleway leading down from Suzanne's Riding School at the top is a dead end. The track below it is a footpath, which, according to Harrow borough engineers, may one day become a bridleway, but not in the foreseeable future. On the back of the research, we have asked Harrow Council to keep the idea alive.

Distance	21km
Grade	Medium – hilly
Bike	Mountain bike
Suitable for children/beginners?	Just about, but the off-road riding is tough, and there are a couple of busy roads
Traffic and surface	20 per cent traffic-free, 20 per cent natural or gravelled surface
Start and finish	Pinner underground station
Overground stations	Headstone Lane
Underground stations	Northwood, Pinner
Refreshments	Pubs and cafés in Pinner High Street, the Boxtree (Boxtree Lane), the Hare (top of Brookhill), the Case is Altered (top of Harrow Weald), the True Lovers Knot (near Copse Wood on A404)
What to see	Old Pinner High Street, Pinner Park Farm, stable buildings of Suzanne's Riding School, Pinner House, Ruislip Lido, views and greenery

1 From Pinner station drop to the main road, and take the first right up Pinner High Street with its half-timbered buildings and smart cafés. In front of the church at the top, turn right into Church Lane, passing 19th-century Pinner House on your left. Turn left at the grassy triangle with the drinking fountain in the middle and left at the top, and take the first right, Wakehams Hill.

Turning off the road into Park Wood, Ruislip.

2 At the top, Nower Hill, take the track on the left (ignore the illegible sign), cross the field on the bridleway and continue to the road (A404). Cross over and continue on the farm road (bridleway) through Pinner Park Farm. Where the track finishes, turn right, signed Headstone Lane and Station. Continue to the road, and turn left carefully, watching for traffic, and, with care, take the first right into Long Elmes.

3 Head up Long Elmes, go straight ahead at the roundabout and take the first left up Boxtree Lane. Continue past the Boxtree pub on your left and take the third left after 100m into Belsize Road. At the dual carriageway at the end, Uxbridge Road, cross carefully to turn right up the hill. At the roundabout at the top, turn left into Brookshill and climb for 1km to the traffic-light junction at the Hare pub.

The attractive off-road track up this hill is part footpath, so cyclists have to climb on the fast road. Nor are we allowed along the picturesque private road, designated a footpath, that leads to Suzanne's Riding School at the top and cuts the corner to Old Redding.

4 Turn left into Old Redding. Head along for 1.5km, past the picnic site, and down to the roundabout. Turn right carefully and take the first left into Royston Park Road. Continue to the end, then turn left and after 20m take the path on the right between the houses that leads over the railway bridge, which has steep steps. On the far side, emerge from the track up the steps between the houses and go left, around the corner beside the school, the road becoming Colburn Avenue, to the T-junction with Hillview Road. Turn right and right again into Grimsdyke Road.

At the end of Grimsdyke Road, walk the bike between the houses. Stay ahead down Staplefield Close and then continue straight on along Albury Drive for another 100m.

5 Keep an eye open for the concreted bridleway on the right signed Pinnerwood Farm and Stud, and turn into it. Continue to the track junction. Here, turn left on the bridleway for Pinner Wood. Get ready for a sandy climb and stay straight ahead, ignoring cross tracks, all the way up through the woods and the golf course.

Mabel and Daisy of Pinner Park Farm.

Bridleway down from Nower Hill.

6 Emerge on a pebbled road, opulent Pinner Hill, continue, and take the second right, Hillside Road, dropping down to the junction with Potter Street. Turn right and continue straight ahead for 1.5km on Hillside Road, becoming Northwood Way and Green Lane, past Northwood underground station and on to the traffic lights with Rickmansworth Road.

7 Turn left and take the first right after 20m into Copse Wood Way. Take the first left into Links Way and at the end enter Ruislip Woods, also known as Copse Wood. Take the bridleway hard right along the edge of the woods against the houses. (There are other bridleways marked on the signboard in Ruislip Woods which you can ride.) Watch out for galloping horses! Continue along a hard sandy climb to the main road and turn left, watching for traffic.

Continue for 1.5km, past the entrance to Ruislip Lido. Just past the BP garage and junction, keep a look out on the left for the bridleway entrance to Park Wood behind a green metal barrier.

8 Enter the woods. Turn right after 20m, and take the gravelled left fork to stay on the main track and bridleway. Continue on this track, ignoring cross tracks and following hoofprints, for 1.5km in more or less a straight line to emerge at Fore Street.

9 Turn right and continue for 300m, then take Wentworth Drive on your left. At the end, turn right, continue to the roundabout then turn left at the mini-roundabout into Eastcote High Road. Continue for 1km, round the big left-hand bend and up the hill, to turn right into High View. At the end go right into West End Lane, and take the second left on a right-hand bend, Chapel Lane, to return to Pinner Station.

Colne Valley Scamper

This charming towpath and bridleway ride starting from Denham Country Park features a piece of good single-track (better before it was gravelled for the horses) and yields rural peace which Londoners usually only dream about. The route passes through the Colne Valley Regional Park, established in the 1960s to improve and safeguard the countryside to the west of London, and for much of the time follows the Colne Valley Trail. The charity Groundwork and the ten local authorities involved are developing new routes for cyclists and walkers.

Bird and canal life thrives alongside the Grand Union Canal where it finally begins its journey northwards. Old gravel pits *en route* are now Sites of Special Scientific Interest, with picturesque narrowboat yards and plenty of tempting watering-holes. Please keep to the Waterways Code for Cyclists (see page 10).

We give two alter native routes. The shorter 6km ride is ideal for children, as it is all flat and mostly off-road.

Distance	17km or 6km
Grade	Long route: medium, with some steep banks; short route: easy, all flat
Bike	Mountain bike
Suitable for children/beginners?	Yes, especially the short circuit, which is mostly off-road
Traffic and surface	75 per cent off-road, with a short stretch of busy road
Start and finish	Colne Valley Regional Park Centre, which is in Denham Country Park, east of Denham. Follow signs along Denham Court Road from the roundabout that feeds the A40/M40 junction
Overground stations	Denham
Underground stations	Rickmansworth, Uxbridge
Refreshments	Visitor Centre, Denham Lock café, the Horse and Barge (Moorhall Road), Black Jack's Mill (near South Harefield), the Fisheries Inn (Harefield), village pubs in Denham
What to see	Denham and Black Jack's Locks, birdlife, canoeists playing in the mill stream at Harefield

1 Starting at Colne Valley Regional Park Centre, from the signposted track 'cross-roads' just off the east (right-hand) side of the road, take the left-hand bridleway and follow it around the fenced paddock. At the end, turn left into the trees, marked 'permissive horseride', and stay on the track for a few hundred metres. Cross the wooden bridge over the River Colne and stay straight ahead. Follow this twisting surfaced track for a few hundred metres, then watch out for your right turn, signed 'Denham Quarry permissive horseride', and follow that up to the canal and Bridge 182. Turn right for a worthwhile diversion southwards to pretty Denham Lock and café.

2 From the lock, retrace your steps northwards up the towpath back to bridge 182.

3 Cross over Bridge 182 to the other side, and continue northwards along a driveway track between the canal and the quarries, marked the Quarry Trail. Continue for 1km to the road, via the driveway under the railway arch and around a narrowboat yard. After a left-hand bend, take the bridleway on the left through the wooden chicane marked Colne Valley Trail, and follow that gravel track past the picnic tables and watery view, out through the Denham Quarry car park to Moorhall Road.

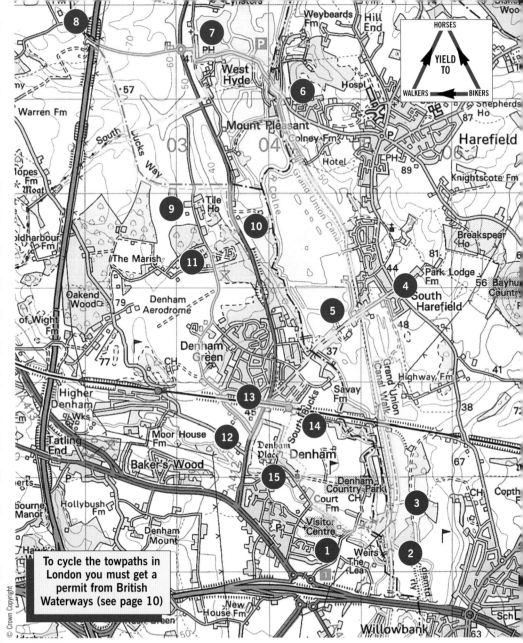

To cycle the towpaths in
London you must get a
permit from British
Waterways (see page 10)

4 The shorter route diverges just past this point.
Turn left on to Moorhall Road, and keep on it
for about 1.4km back into the built-up area. At the
crossroads before the main A412 turn left into
Savay Lane, then right into Savay Close. At the end
pick up the path behind the houses that leads

under the viaduct beneath the station. Rejoin the
longer ride at point 14.

5 For the longer route, turn left on to Moorhall
Road. After 350m, opposite the Horse and Barge
pub and barbecue garden, and Harefield Marina,

turn right carefully into the lane signposted for the quarry. Stay on this track, with the towpath out of sight on the right and the reservoir bird reserves on the left, for 1.5km as far as bridge 178 and Black Jack's lock and restaurant.

Cross over to the other side of the canal and turn left into Jack's Lane, signed Colne Valley Trail (and legal for bikes even though it's a footpath). Follow this, now with the canal on your left for 800m, past smart new canalside housing as far as the road. Turn left downhill to the lights and cross over the bridge beside the Fisheries Inn.

6 Continue along the road, Coppermill Lane, for 1km to the T-junction at the Fisherman's Tackle pub.

7 For a short-cut saving 2km, turn left at the Fisherman's Tackle. After 400m take the bridleway marked No. 4 on the right before the white house. Follow that straight ahead across the A412 and up the field.

For the main route, follow the road round to the right, turn left shortly to the main road. Watch the traffic as you go straight ahead over the roundabout on the A412, then climb for 1km up the narrow lane.

8 At the M25 bridge at the top, take the roller-coaster single-track bridleway left that leads for 2km along a hedgerow into the distance. Watch out for horses and walkers.

9 Cross a lane after 2km and keep on the bridleway as it heads downhill. At the bottom where you meet the A412, turn right, either on the road or along the verge for 500m.

10 Turn right up the hill on a leafy, rooted bridleway, which is tough work and slippery in the wet, for 300m.

11 Turn left on to the road at the end, and continue for 2km back downhill to the main A412 past the runway of Denham Aerodrome.

12 At the A412 at the bottom, watching the traffic, turn left towards the railway bridge. Use the road or the grass verge, or walk your bike along the pathway.

13 Beyond the railway bridge, turn right immediately up Denham Station Road. Go on to the platform, walk down the subway steps and emerge underneath the station viaduct arch.

Turn right on to the track. (The shorter ride rejoins here.)

14 Around the corner of the arch, on the right-hand bend, go between the wooden fencing to get on to the straight mud track for 400m. Do not take the parallel tarmac track, which is a footpath (curiously named The Pyghtle).

15 For a short-cut in muddy weather, divert through quaint Denham village. At the end of The Pyghtle continue straight ahead, keeping the brick wall to your right. Turn left through the high street, and after 200m, following a hard right-hand corner over the river, turn left on the road to get back to the Visitor Centre.

The main route follows the circular bridleway of the Colne Valley park, marked variously 'bridleway', 'permissive footpath' and 'permissive horseride'. At the end of The Pyghtle, turn left on the track and stick to it for 1.5km back to the Visitor Centre, around Buckinghamshire golf course, past Denham church and cemetery, turning left and right through the ornate gate of the golf club and continuing through fields and woods back along the River Misbourne.

For a leaflet showing three gentler routes, write to Colne Valley Park Centre, Denham Court Drive, Denham UB9 5PG; tel: 01895 833375

Cross over the canal at Black Jack's Lock.

View from the bridge at Harefield.

ROUTE 21

Western Water Tour

Do not underestimate this mountain-bike trip through the west London suburbs. It may be mostly on towpath, but at 38km, with lots to look at and plenty of watering holes, it forms a substantial ride. Rich scenes of life on the water – houseboats, herons and rowers – reveal themselves as you progress west along the Paddington branch of the Grand Union Canal. Then the route turns east along the main canal, through the Brent River Nature Reserve, and on to the elegant reaches of the urban Thames. A 4km-stretch on roads, past the back of Wormwood Scrubs nick, closes the circle.

Distance	38km
Grade	Medium – flat but long
Bike	Preferably with knobbly tyres
Suitable for children/beginners?	Yes, because the ride is largely off-road. But it is a long haul on knobbly tyres and the roads between the Thames at Hammersmith and the canal at Harlesden are busy
Traffic and surface	85 per cent traffic-free; 29km of towpath, rough in places
Start and finish	Mitre Bridge on Scrubs Lane, Harlesden, or to suit. The places where you can join the canal towpath are marked on the map
Overground stations	Barnes Bridge, Brentford, Greenford, Gunnersbury, Hayes & Harlington, Kew Bridge, Stonebridge Park, Willesden Junction. At Greenford, Stonebridge Park and Willesden Junction you cannot take your bike on to the underground that uses the same or the adjacent station
Underground stations	Goldhawk Road, Gunnersbury, Hammersmith, Ladbroke Grove, Ravenscourt Park, Shepherds Bush (Hammersmith & City Line only), Stamford Brook
Refreshments	Canal and river pubs: the Black Horse (Oldfield Road, Greenford), Grand Junction Arms (Western Road, Southall), the Fox (Green Lane, Hanwell), the Black Lion (Black Lion Lane, Hammersmith)
What to see	Herons, the flight of locks at Hanwell, Brent River Nature Reserve, canal and river life

1 Starting at Mitre Bridge on Scrubs Lane in Harlesden, turn westwards on to the towpath of the Grand Union Canal. Continue for 15km along the towpath to Bull's Bridge Junction.

This is the Paddington arm of the Grand Union Canal, which was built in 1801 and continues east alongside London Zoo and through Camden Town, Islington and Hackney to reach the Thames at Limehouse. The scene is fairly urban as the Canal passes over the North Circular Road and through Alperton, which flourished in the 19th century as a brick- and tile-making centre.

2 The towpath becomes unsurfaced and more interesting for 2km below 84m-high Horsenden Hill, where countryside takes over. Here on the left is Perivale Wood, established in 1902–04 as a 27-acre nature reserve rich in oak and hazel and home to over seventy species of birds.

3 Some 3km further on, just before passing beneath the A40, note the new mosque at the footbridge. After another 1km, the name and logo of Taylor Woodrow are spelt out in brickwork on the left bank, opposite the company works in Taywood Road. Another 1km on, an area once dotted with numerous canal arms and basins serving brickfields and factories has been landscaped to form the Willowtree Marina and Chandlery, which opens out on the far side of the canal.

4 Bull's Bridge Junction is the meeting-point of the Paddington branch and the main Grand Union Canal. The ride turns east (left) here, and

To cycle the towpaths in London you must get a permit from British Waterways – and please follow the Waterways Code for Cyclists (see page 10).

♦ access to canal/river

© Crown Copyright

ROUTE
21

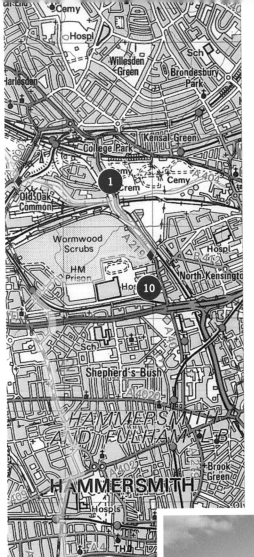

continues along the Canal as far as the Thames at Brentford. At Three Bridges on Windmill Lane, three modes of transport intersect: the canal, a road and a deep-cut railway line, built by Isambard Kingdom Brunel.

5 The ride's most spectacular feature is the flight of six locks at Hanwell. These raise the Canal by 20 metres in 200m, and represent the only real height change along the route. Watch for people, children and dogs – it's easy to speed down here.

Below the last lock is the confluence of the Canal and the River Brent, which has made its way through north London. The towpath now follows the meandering river for another 4km to the Thames, through the chain of reclaimed meadows and scrubland of Brent River Nature Reserve. Watch out, say the signboards, for little grebes, grey wagtails and kingfishers. Other sights are Osterley Lock, the high green girders supporting the M4 motorway, the iron railway bridge that carries Piccadilly Line underground trains, and the handsome span of Gallows Bridge, which switches the towpath to the south bank.

Finally the route passes through a large disused boathouse, and emerges at Brentford Lock on to the A315, Brentford High Street.

Hanwell Locks: industrial history in the suburbs

The confluence of the Grand Union Canal (left) and Brent River (right) at the bottom of Hanwell Locks.

6 If you have time, it is worth exploring Brent Dock, a smart estate on the spit where the canal and River Brent flow into the Thames, with boathouses, wharves and inlets. Take the first right from the High Street into Augustus Close, and leave the estate by Dock Road.

Otherwise, at Brentford Lock, turn left, eastwards, and follow the A315 through Brentford, past Waterman's Arts Centre, the Musical Museum and Kew Bridge Steam Museum (see ride 12) to Kew Bridge. The riverside path is interrupted through Brentford, so ignore the signs to it unless you want a dead-end look at the river.

7 At the traffic lights at Kew Bridge, get carefully into the centre lane and cross straight ahead into little Strand on the Green, becoming Thames Road. Note that cycling is not allowed along the pretty riverfront parallel with these roads. So walk or lock up your bike to enjoy the riverside and visit the pleasant local pubs.

Continue straight ahead for just over 1km. Thames Road becomes Grove Road and then Hartington Road. At the crossing with Great Chertsey Road, cross straight over and follow the cycle signs on the road that runs along the riverbank for 1km.

8 Stay with the tarmac beneath Barnes Bridge (railway), and follow the cycle signs for 1km to a roundabout at Corney Reach at a new riverside housing development. There go right/straight ahead for 1km, along Pumping Station Road and on to Chiswick Mall. This is a popular walkway, so mind the people. Pass along the 18th-century terrace at the end to the Black Lion pub.

The riverside path continues past long-established riverside pubs to ornate Hammersmith Bridge, done up in Harrods livery (a reference perhaps to the Harrods Depository just beyond it on the south bank?). This is worth a wander, but cycling is not officially allowed, so push or lock up the bike.

9 To return to the start of the ride, at the Black Lion pub we swap the water for 4km of roads northwards back to the Canal at Harlesden.

Turn left along South Black Lion Lane, then take the subway beneath the A4. On the far side, turn left into elegant St Peter's Square, staying with it

and turning right at the end. At the main road, King Street, turn left and immediately right at the lights into Goldhawk Road. Continue along here for 500m, around the bend, and take the first true left, Ashchurch Park Villas. Take the right at the end, Ashchurch Terrace, to gain Askew Road, where you turn left. Continue northwards to the lights at the junction with Uxbridge Road, and go straight ahead.

After 600m, just before the big junction with Westway, turn right carefully into Hilary Road, and then left at the end. Cross Westway at the bike lights, and go straight ahead, still along Hilary Road. Dog-leg left to continue in the same direction up Fitzneal Street, and take the first right, Erconwald Street.

10 At the end, turn right into Braybrook Street, and after 50m left on to Wormwood Scrubs beside the prison walls. Continue for 1km beside the prison, through the hospital carpark and around the dilapidated Linford Christie stadium, to pick up Scrubs Lane. Turn left up the hill and after 600m you hit the canal bridge.

View along to Hammersmith Bridge. After 2km of lovely riverside riding, the route turns inland here.

On the Canal at Alperton.

Chessington Chase

This gentle circuit uses Chessington World of Adventures as a pivot, and provides a good introduction to mountain biking for children and for less fit adults. At just 12km long, the route is mostly off-road, but follows many made-up tracks with reliable surfaces.

Please walk your bike on the section across Claygate Common. This is a 'permissive horseride' only, but it's worth pushing the bike to avoid a road diversion.

Take care, particularly with children, on the stretch along the busy A243, and use the footpath if you prefer. This section is unavoidable because the Crown Estate allows horses and walkers but not cyclists on the direct track through Prince's Coverts between the A243 and the B280. On the back of the research for this ride the Crown Estate was asked in September 1997 to consider letting cyclists use the Prince's Coverts track in the future. The reply from the chief forester ran: 'Allowing general access for cycling, which these days invariably means mountain biking, would not accord with our access policy. The management problems we are currently experiencing on the Windsor Estate from the cycling sector make it extremely unlikely that we shall change the policy for Oxshott Estate.'

Distance	12km
Grade	Easy – largely off-road but mostly on made-up tracks
Bike	Mountain bike
Suitable for children/beginners?	Yes. There is a lot of nice off-road riding, but the section on the A243 is dodgy
Traffic and surface	85 per cent good off-road
Start and finish	Car park at Horton Country Park, north-west of Epsom
Overground stations	Chessington South, Epsom, Ewell West
Refreshments	The Star, Leatherhead Road (borough cycling officer's recommendation!), the Cricketers pub on Epsom Common and eateries in Epsom town centre
What to see	Horton Country Park, the woodland skirts of Ashtead National Nature Reserve
What to visit	Chessington World of Adventures theme park

Neddy and Bob of the stables on Kingston Road.

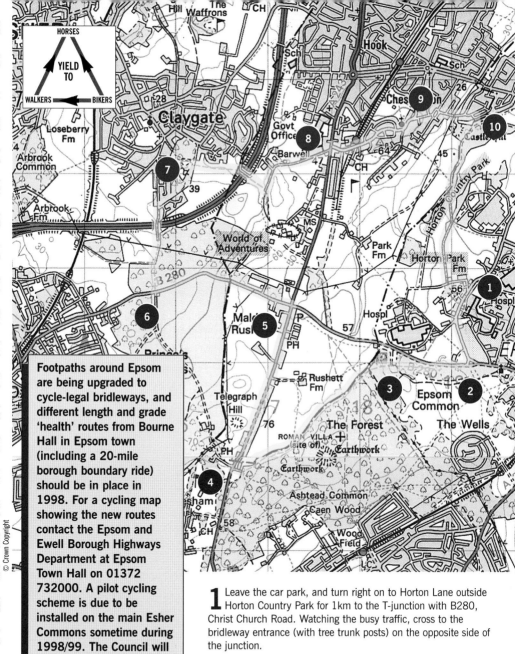

HORSES
YIELD TO
WALKERS ← → BIKERS

© Crown Copyright

Footpaths around Epsom are being upgraded to cycle-legal bridleways, and different length and grade 'health' routes from Bourne Hall in Epsom town (including a 20-mile borough boundary ride) should be in place in 1998. For a cycling map showing the new routes contact the Epsom and Ewell Borough Highways Department at Epsom Town Hall on 01372 732000. A pilot cycling scheme is due to be installed on the main Esher Commons sometime during 1998/99. The Council will monitor use for a year before deciding whether to allow cycling permanently – so it's over to you.

1 Leave the car park, and turn right on to Horton Lane outside Horton Country Park for 1km to the T-junction with B280, Christ Church Road. Watching the busy traffic, cross to the bridleway entrance (with tree trunk posts) on the opposite side of the junction.

2 Follow the bridleway to the right, westwards, for 1km, following signs for Chessington Country Walk. Continue past a little white-painted wooden bridge and a pond, and then pick up the bridleway along the boundary of Ashtead Common National Nature Reserve.

3 Following the blue-tipped posts, continue along this boundary bridleway, signposted Kingston Road, for 1.5 km. Keep straight ahead at all bridleway junctions. Eventually leave the nature reserve between a stables and paddock to reach the A243.

4 Take care as you turn right on to the very busy road – use the footpath if you prefer or if you have children with you – and follow it for 1.6km to the crossroads with the B280, where you turn left towards Malden Rushett.

5 Continue along this road for 1.6km to a bridleway crossing at the gated entrance to Prince's Coverts. Turn right on to the bridleway and continue, watching out for logging work in progress, across the bridge over the dual-carriageway A3. Take the first right, Holroyd Road, continue for 100m, then turn off where the road bends to the right on to Claygate Common marked 'Horse Ride'. Please walk your bike from here (marked with a dashed line), following the arrows. Take care to mind the horses. This is a popular permissive horseride where cyclists currently have no right to ride.

6 Remount after 800m, where a line of half-timbered houses begins. Turn right, climb briefly, cross the A3 again by bridge, and continue on the bridleway straight ahead. After 200m turn left (Chessington World of Adventures lies beyond the brow of this hill), and follow this bridleway for 1km as it joins tarmac beside a farm and veers eastwards to the main road. Watch out for the camouflaged speed bumps!

7 Cross straight over the A243, and pass into Garrison Lane for 1km, past Chessington South station, then St Mary the Virgin parish church, where the road becomes Church Lane. Soon after, turn right into Stokesby Road.

8 At the elongated grass roundabout, take the opposite exit, Filby Road, and continue for 800m, as it becomes Rollesby Road. Ignore the signs for Horton Country Park. Between house numbers 102 and 100 turn right off the road and enter Horton Country Park to the left behind the garages, between the right-hand metal pole barrier.

9 Inside the Park, take the main cindered track straight ahead for 200m, then, at a four-way junction, turn right on to the bigger, embanked track. Keep straight ahead where the woodland opens out, and after another 500m fork left between wooden fencing, following signs for Chessington Country Walk and Thames Down Link. After 200m, at the edge of the park, turn right and climb gently for the last 800m, gaining the edge of Epsom Polo Club, back to the Country Park car park.

Spring comes to Claygate Common

Epsom Gallop

This fascinating mountain-bike ride is steeped in equestrian culture, crossing Epsom racecourse and making the most of the myriad tracks around the pleasant little Surrey town. Although it is not particularly long, the route is not for beginners. Up on Epsom Down the wind blows strongly and the climb beyond it to Walton on the Hill is hard, especially after rain. However, these riding tests are balanced by the flatness and tranquillity of Ashtead Common and Forest, designated a National Nature Reserve, and home to some two thousand centuries-old oaks that form a unique habitat for plants and invertebrates.

It is crucial to remember that racehorses are much more nervous than your average horse. You must follow mountain bike etiquette to the letter, and stop or yield to them at all times on the bridleways and gallops. The short section of road along Church Lane in Headley village is tight, and carries a lot of horse-box traffic, so ride it with your eyes and ears open.

Distance	19km
Grade	Medium to difficult – not too long, but with one hard climb
Bike	Mountain bike
Suitable for children/beginners?	No for beginners. Yes for experienced children, but it is a tough off-road ride, and you must take care through Headley village
Traffic and surface	80 per cent off-road, lots of natural surface, potentially very muddy
Start and finish	Epsom station
Overground stations	Epsom, Tattenham Corner
Refreshments	Pubs – the Amato (Chalk Lane, Epsom), the Rubbing House on Epsom racecourse, the Cock Horse in Headley village, the Cricketers on Epsom Common village green
What to see	Epsom racecourse, with the view to London, stables and gallops

1 Turn right at the mini-roundabout outside Epsom station (Waterloo Road). At the first set of lights go straight ahead (over the High Street) into the one-way system. In the left-hand lane stay straight ahead, going on into Ashley Road. At the corner of Rosebery Park, take the path into the park and continue past the pond and along the wooden fencing. Cross Avenue Road and go straight ahead into Madans Walk. At the end, turn left up Chalk Lane.

Take the vehicle track across Epsom racecourse.

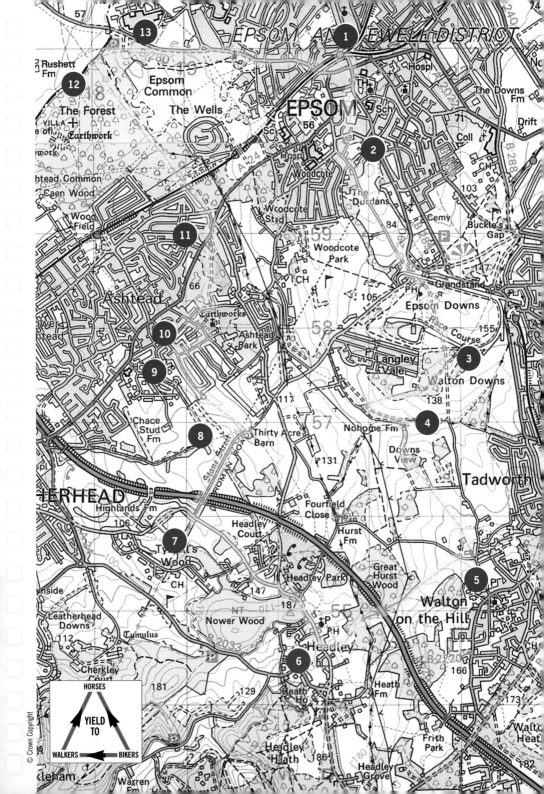

2 Chalk Lane climbs to the top of Epsom Downs in 1km, emerging near the spectacular Grandstand. (For a fine view back to London, divert left at the T-junction with the B290 and ride along it eastwards for 200m or so to a car park viewpoint that names the buildings you can see.)

Just before the road junction, take the grey-white hard-top track, right, that leads over the top of the road, across the nearside race track itself and alongside the pub, the Rubbing House. Then take the bridleway that leads directly across the race course. Watch out for horses training.

3 After crossing the farside race track, continue straight ahead for 200m, then turn right at a four-way track junction beyond the white metal pole barrier. After 300m watch carefully on a right-hand bend for the single track, marked bridleway, that turns off left. Pass through the trees, ignoring a crossing track, and drop down the open grass slope, bearing 45 degrees to the right, to the track at the bottom. Turn left and continue to the house, Nohome Farm. Watch out for horses training.

4 Take the single-track bridleway that rises beside the left of the house and prepare for a tough, tricky 1.5km climb, especially if it is muddy. Ride to the end of the tarmac and turn right.

5 After 150m, at the 'Mid-Surrey Pony Club' sign, turn left between fields to enjoy an 800m descent. Continue under the M25 motorway and stay straight ahead on the double-track bridleway for 800m to Headley village road.

6 Turn right on to this road, Church Lane, and ride along it through the village, past the Cock Horse pub. Take special care here, as there have been many accidents involving cars, and there is no footway on which you can take refuge. After 800m take the left turn, signposted Leatherhead, past RAF Headley.

7 After 1km, just before a chevroned bend, watch carefully on the right for the turning for the Stane Street double track, and head along it. Cross the motorway again and continue straight ahead for 1km along the double track, ignoring the bridleway junction, to the white-painted Thirty Acre Barn stables (belonging to the most successful trainer in the area, Geoff Lewis).

8 Here, turn left along the single-track bridleway for 500m. At the end continue straight ahead on to the gravel road for 500m to the first junction.

9 Turn right into Chalk Lane, and ride for 500m to the end of the road, opposite the Corporation of London Freemen's School.

10 Turn left on to the road. Then, at the first junction, turn right through the white gates of Ashtead Park estate. After 300m, opposite the back entrance of the school, turn left and continue straight ahead through the park under the height restriction bar. After 700m, leave the estate at the white gates on the busy A24 Epsom–Leatherhead road. Turn right with care, and after 100m take the first left into Craddocks Avenue.

11 The next bridleway comes soon on the right, beside the sign announcing that you are entering Ashtead National Nature Reserve. Follow the blue-tipped posts for 2km, taking care across the railway level-crossing. Keep more or less straight ahead, ignoring cross-tracks.

12 When you reach a bridleway junction near farmland, turn right, marked for Epsom Common. After 200m, at the five-way track crossing, continue ahead, signposted Chessington Countryside Walk. Pass a pond on your right and stay on the track, now also marked Winter Horseride and Thames Down Link.

13 On reaching the road, ignore the paths turning left over the little white-painted bridge and stay on the bridleway parallel to the road eastwards for 1km. Take your pick of bridleway tracks around the back of Christ Church. Move on to the road near Epsom Common village green (the Cricketers pub) and continue into Epsom.

The route through Rosebery Park from Epsom town centre towards the Downs.

Valleys and Views around Warlingham

This meaty, muddy, rural mountain-bike ride up and down the approach valleys of the North Downs touches the most southerly point of all the routes in this book. It's a pretty ride, but not for beginners, as you need to be fit and have a degree of handling ability for the good single-track climbs and descents.

Nearly half the ride is off-road on parts of the area's abundant bridleway network, so you will come across plenty of horseriders and walkers in good weather, to whom you should show the usual courtesies of stopping or yielding. We got a bit of angry lip from one horseman who had recently had trouble with speeding cyclists, while from others we had friendly greetings. The law (Section 30 of the 1968 Countryside Act) does allow cycles on bridleways, so quote it – politely – if your right to be on any of these bridleways is challenged.

One steep bridleway (point 5 on the map) spits you out on the road from a steep descent. So we recommend staying on the road route described at this point unless you are an experienced descender.

1 Start at the car park at the top of the steep grassy slopes of Riddlesdown. Follow the track out of the end of the car park for 500m, then leave the down to the left at the Corporation of London sign at the houses. Turn right along Honister Heights, sign-posted bridleway. At the end of the houses, go off-road again, on the bridleway signed for Hamsey Green. Follow this through trees and across open fields for 1.5km, ignoring the footpath fork off to the right after 1km.

2 At the road go straight ahead along Tithepit Shaw Lane for 500m, then cross straight over the main road and head down Kingswood Lane. After 500m, take the right turn, at the overgrown sign for the bridleway to Farleigh Common, towards the stables. Stop or yield to all the horses you meet. Take the bridleway to the left of the stables, and follow that through the trees along the edge of the field. Watch for horses all the way for 1km and control your speed down the little dale.

Emerge at Farleigh Road, turn right, and after 300m turn left opposite the Harrow pub. After 300m, at the end of the houses, turn left again, up Daniels Lane, and take the right-hand bridleway at the end. Watch for horses all the way along here. After 150m, watch for the track on the left that leads along the edge of the field, and take that, ignoring the tracks that continue into Greatpark Wood. Keep

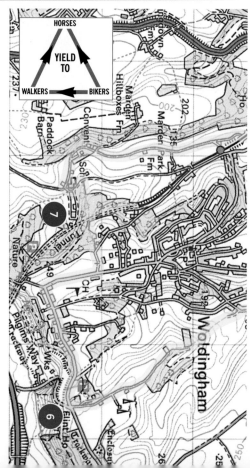

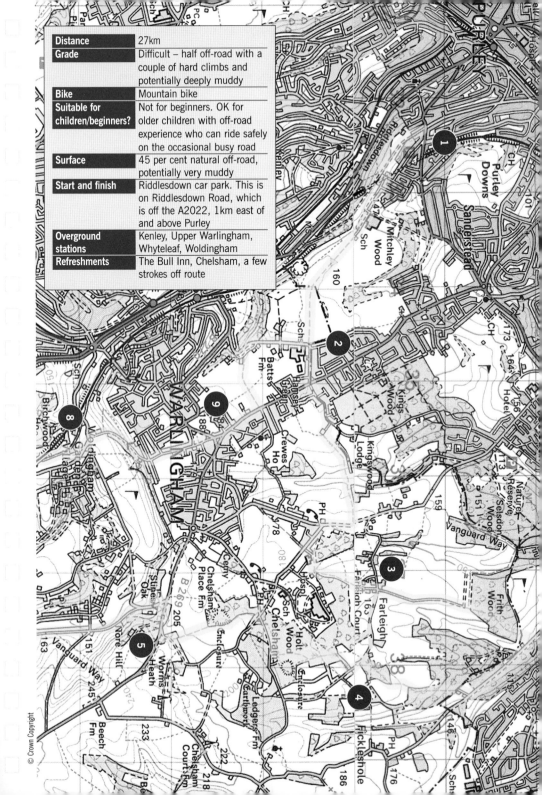

Distance	27km
Grade	Difficult – half off-road with a couple of hard climbs and potentially deeply muddy
Bike	Mountain bike
Suitable for children/beginners?	Not for beginners. OK for older children with off-road experience who can ride safely on the occasional busy road
Surface	45 per cent natural off-road, potentially very muddy
Start and finish	Riddlesdown car park. This is on Riddlesdown Road, which is off the A2022, 1km east of and above Purley
Overground stations	Kenley, Upper Warlingham, Whyteleaf, Woldingham
Refreshments	The Bull Inn, Chelsham, a few strokes off route

© Crown Copyright

to the edge of the wood to Farleigh Court and St Mary's Church, where there are stables and you must yield to the horses.

3 For a 3km short-cut here, turn right, follow the road, and rejoin the route at point 4.

For the longer main route, cross over Farleigh Court Road into the double-track beside the golf course and follow that for 1km, to the start of Frith Wood. Continue straight ahead into the trees and enjoy a nice descent, but control your speed and watch for horses and people all the way. Emerge at Featherbed Lane, opposite Farleigh Dean Crescent, and turn right. Continue along the road for 1km (on past the scout camp) and then turn right carefully – the cars come downhill round the bend towards you – into the bridleway beside Pear Tree Farm.

The ride is now off-road again, and there's a stiff single-track climb up through Crab Wood, where you go straight ahead all the way, ignoring cross-tracks, for 800m as far as a grassy fork. Continue on the right-hand track, cross Little Farleigh Green on the track parallel with the white house and continue to the road, Scotshall Lane.

4 Turn left along the road for 200m, then take the bridleway on the right through the metal gate. At the end of the single-track straight, stay on the main track, which bears left and becomes double-track. Continue on this track, through Holt Wood, to emerge at the road, Church Lane, beside the cluster of buildings called The Holt. Turn right and continue to the little cross-roads (the Bull Inn at Chelsham is ahead and to the right), and take the gated bridleway off-road on the left through the trees just beyond. Follow this for 1km, as far as Ledgers Road. There, turn right briefly and turn right again on to the B269 Limpsfield Road.

5 After 150m turn left down steep Slines Oak Road.

(A steep downhill bridleway cuts off this corner. However, it drops you fast out on to Slines Oak Road, and so it must only be ridden – with care – by experienced bikers. This route is as follows: 100m after turning on to to the B269, turn left up the bridleway-signed driveway marked Private Road. After 50m, beyond the white garage, look carefully on the right for the narrow entrance of the single-track bridleway. Control your speed all the way down and slow down before you are spat out on to the road at the bottom. Watch for people and horses. Turn left at the road).

Continue for 1km along Slines Oak Road. Then, where the road curves right, take the wide track straight ahead, with a lovely, grassy 100m climb up the open hillside in full view. Prepare to grind! At the top, continue for 1km along the double-track to the T-junction and turn right into the Ridge.

6 Follow the road for 2km, continuing round the right-hand bend where it becomes Northdown Road. Watch on the left for rough, little Church Road. Follow that for 200m and then, on the right-hand corner, take the bridleway straight ahead. This is another rough descent, through Great Church Wood Nature Reserve and on all the way to the bottom of the valley, so control your speed all the way down and watch for people and horses. After 300m turn right at the first track T-junction, then, after passing over the top of the railway tunnel after 400m at the second track T-junction, turn left.

7 Pick up the road and follow it round the school buildings to the right, then turn right on to the valley road and continue between more school buildings, along the pretty valley bottom for 2km. 300m after passing under the railway bridge, just where the trees start at the top of a little rise, look out for an opening on the right and take the short single-track bridleway off-road between the hedges and around the wood. Continue to Woldingham Road and turn left.

8 At the road junction after 200m, take the little road for Warlingham straight ahead up the 800m climb of Bug Hill, where the boy racers like to test their engine power. At the top, stay with the road as it flattens, becoming Leas Road, and continue to the junction with Hillbury Road, where you turn right briefly. Turn left, joining the traffic around the Green at Warlingham, and continue straight ahead along Limpsfield Road.

9 After 500m, opposite Crewe Lane, take the bridleway off-road to the left and follow that for 600m to the end. Emerge on a little side road above the main road and go left. At the end, turn right, with great care, on to Tithepit Shaw Lane, and continue for 800m, back to the corner at point number 2. Turn left off-road again and retrace your pedalstrokes 3km back to Riddlesdown.

Cresting the biggest climb in the book, 100m up the hill at Woldingham.

Big Air at Biggin Hill

This hilly route represents a fine piece of 'London' mountain biking, just 15 miles south of the city centre and 30 minutes' train journey from the central stations. You will find it a demanding and satisfying ride. Lanes link stretches of bridleway rich in pastoral sights and sounds – lambs in spring, tractors on the road, and the crop cycle – while the magnificent views from the North Downs are of deepest Kent and Surrey.

The second half features climbs and descents that need strength and stamina – hence the 'difficult' tag. The best are on the slopes of a beautiful, nameless valley of green sward to the west of Biggin Hill and Tatsfield.

Distance	29km
Grade	Difficult – hilly, and also tough after wet weather, especially the second half
Bike	Mountain bike
Suitable for children/beginners?	No problem with traffic, but this is a rough off-road ride
Traffic and surface	50 per cent traffic-free, 50 per cent natural; potentially very muddy
Start and finish	Byway from the A21 on the edge of Chelsfield, near the roundabout junction with the A223
Overground stations	Chelsfield, Orpington
Refreshments	Cafés in Orpington; the Blacksmith's Arms, Cudham; the Tea Cosy teashop in Downe village
What to see	Views of Kent and Surrey from the North Downs ridge, the 'secret' valley, pretty Downe village
What to visit	Down House, Downe village (closed Mondays and Tuesdays, and all February)

1 Climb the byway that leads off right just beyond the A21 roundabout on the outskirts of Chelsfield, up through fields and woods, turning left after 1km at the houses.

2 Turn left again after 300m along the byway sign-posted Knockholt Pound and Pratts Bottom, which undulates (hence the wooden speed bars) for 2km, forking right at the wire fence after a few hundred metres and then left at the top of the logged climb to reach the road.

3 At the road, turn right and continue for 750m to the white cottage. Then turn right on to the

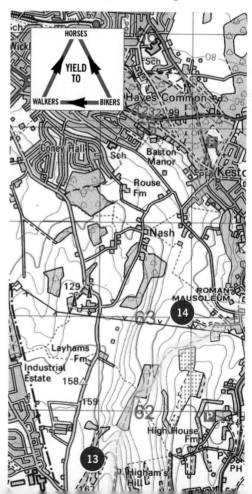

sign-posted bridleway. Follow this short, rough, cambered track to the road, and turn right again.

4 Continue along this road to the T-junction at Cudham, and turn right for 300m. Then, opposite the Blacksmith's Arms, turn left into New Barn Lane, and descend, then climb, for 2km.

5 At the junction with Berrys Green Road, take the sign-posted public bridleway right across the fields. Turn left just before the six-barred metal gate demarking private property, and soon right again in the same direction across fields to the A233.

6 Turn left on to the main road with caution. After 1km, at Hawleys Corner, carefully turn right, sign-posted Tatsfield, and take the left fork along the gravelled road beside the garden centre. Continue for 1km, then, on the left-hand bend at the black-and-white half-timbered house, turn right along the North Downs scarp.

7 Continue for 1km to the four-way junction, turn westwards on to the B2024, and continue for 1km to the right turn, sign-posted Tatsfield, beside the radio mast. Follow this road into Tatsfield.

8 At the Tatsfield village sign, turn left into Lusted Hall Lane, and follow it for 300m to the top of a little dip. There, take the sign-posted bridleway to the left and follow it over the grassy field and down a short, sharp drop. Go up and through the wooden gate, and cut diagonally across the middle of the field to the opposite corner (not along the woodland fence) to the road. Turn right and follow for 300m.

9 Turn left opposite the cottages through a five-bar wooden gate sign-posted bridleway, and follow it diagonally across the field (near the telegraph poles) towards the farm buildings. Now comes the fun bit. Take the double track round

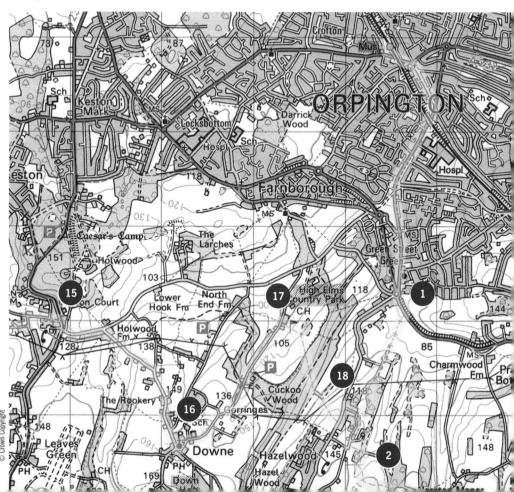

Horse and carriage in Downe village.

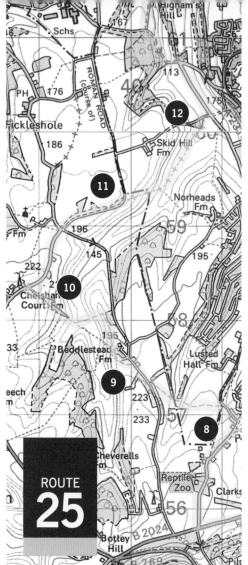

ROUTE
25

the back alongside the conifers and stay with it as it twists, drops to the bottom of a lovely valley, then climbs hard towards the radio mast.

10 At the road, turn right for about 1km. Then, on a chevroned left-hand bend, turn off to the right, sign-posted for Addington and Biggin Hill, and follow the road along the top of the same valley for 1km.

11 On a chevroned bend, turn right off the road on to a fast, descending track. This becomes a road used as a public path (RUPP) that leads all the way back to the bottom of the valley. Control your speed and watch for horses and walkers.

12 At the road at the bottom, turn left for 600m, then left again at the T-junction. Take care up the hard, narrow climbing road where cars can be impatient.

13 Near the top, turn right carefully on to a bridleway (this may be marked Highams

Farm), and continue straight ahead for 2.5km to Keston Court.

14 Leave the track at the farm, where you are asked to ride considerately, and turn left and bear right up the hill, past Keston parish church to emerge at the A233.

15 Turn right then left at the mini-roundabout into Downe Road, and head for pretty Downe village, 2km away.

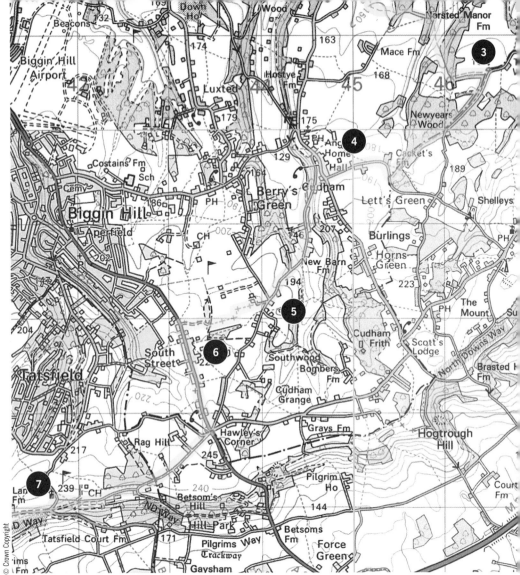

16 In Downe you can stop for refreshments, and also to look at the Darwin Museum in Down House, for 40 years the home of the naturalist Sir Charles Darwin. When you are ready to cycle on, turn left at the church and left again around the back, sign-posted High Elms and Farnborough. (If you pass Christmas Tree Farm, you've gone wrong.) Continue for 1.8km as far as the cottages on the right at the far end of the golf course.

17 Turn right up the bridleway clearly sign-posted Cudham Lane North. This climbs, descends, and climbs hard again to the road.

18 Turn left for 100m, then right up the gravel driveway serving the houses, and rejoin the byway where the ride started.

The bridleway turn-off at Beddlestead Farm, point 9.

Useful addresses

Organisations

Cyclists' Tourist Club (CTC)
– a fount of information on cycle travel, mechanics and politics. Highly credible nationwide campaign group consulted by government. The base for the British mountain bike access campaign work.
Cotterell House
69 Meadrow
Godalming,
Surrey GU7 3HS
Tel: 01483 417217
Fax: 01483 426994

The British Cycling Federation (BCF) incorporating British Mountain Biking
– cycle racing organisation
1 Stuart Street
Manchester M11 4DQ
Tel: 0161-230 2301

The London School of Cycling
– teaches absolute beginner adults to ride bikes in an hour!
147 Amhurst Road
London E8 9NT
Tel: 0171-249 3779
Email: lsc@clara.net

Sustrans
– the charity that builds cycle paths and other facilities for cyclists, creators of the National Cycle Network
35 King Street
Bristol BS1 4DZ
Tel: 0117-929 0888
Fax: 0117-929 4173
Email: sustrans@sustrans.org.uk
Website: www.sustrans.org.uk

London Cycling Campaign (LCC)
– campaigning for a London where everyone can cycle comfortably for transport; 8,000 members and growing.
228 Great Guildford Business Square
30 Great Guildford Street
London SE1 0HS
Tel: 0171-928 7220
Fax: 0171-928 2318
Website: www.lcc.org.uk/lcc/

London Cycling Development Officer, Mark Wyer
– promotes cycling for children and sport in the capital
c/o Southwark Council
15 Spa Road
Bermondsey,
London SE16 3QW
Tel: 0171-525 1539

The Bicycle Association
– the cycle trade organisation
Starley House
Eaton Road
Coventry CV1 2FH
Tel: 01203 553838

British Waterways Board
– for permits to ride the canals and information
The Toll House
Delamere Terrace
Little Venice
London W2 6ND
Tel: 0171-286 6101
Fax: 0171-286 7306

Venues

Herne Hill Stadium
– racing and tuition
Burbage Road
London SE24 9HE
Tel: Southwark Leisure Management on 0171-231 9442

Hillingdon Cycle Circuit
– new tarmac circuit, racing and tuition
Springfield Road
Hayes, Middx
Tel: 0181-737 7797

Lee Valley Cycle Circuit (previously Eastway)
– tarmac track, mtb course and bmx track
Temple Mills Lane
London E15 2EN
Tel: 0181-534 6085
Fax: 0181-536 0959

Books and maps

Bicycling Books
– specialist cycle book distributor
309-311 Horn Lane
London W3 0BU
Tel: 0181-993 3484

Stanfords Map and Book Service
– London's most established map and travel shop, mail order service
12-14 Long Acre
Covent Garden
London WC2E 9LP
Tel: 0171-836 1321
Fax: 0171-836 0189
Email: sales@stanfords.co.uk

Off you go and enjoy yourself!

Author: Nicky Crowther

Editor: Christopher Pick

Location photography: Nicky Crowther

Front cover photograph: Gerard Brown

Designer: Dave Hermelin

Production Manager: Kevin Perrett

Project Manager: Louise McIntyre

Page makeup: Jill Gough

British Library Cataloguing-in-Publication Data:
A catalogue record for this book is available from the British Library.

ISBN 1 85960 320 3

London base maps pages 21-23, 25, 28-29, 35-37, 40-41, 45, 49-50, 55-56, 61, 65-67, 69-71,
74-77, 81, 84-87, 89-91, cover map extract, generated from Bartholomew London Digital database;
and M25 London Orbital Motorway map pages 16-17 © Nicholson 1998. (LG 9893)
Data supplied by HarperCollins Cartographic, Bartholomew Mapping Services, Westerhill Road,
Bishopbriggs. Tel. 0141-306 3180. WWW.harpercollins.co.uk.maps.

Maps reproduced from Ordnance Survey Landranger Mapping with the permission
of the controller of HMSO © Crown Copyright, Licence No. 43373U.